ARCHITECTURE

The 50 most influential architects in the world

First published in Great Britain in 2010

A & C Black Publishers Ltd
36 Soho Square
London W1D 3QY
www.acblack.com

Copyright © Elwin Street Limited 2010

ISBN: 978 1 4081 2001 9

Conceived and produced by
Elwin Street Limited
144 Liverpool Road
London N1 1LA
United Kingdom
www.elwinstreet.com

Design: Louise Leffler at Sticks Design

Picture credits: Alamy: pp.7, 15, 17, 21, 25, 31, 37, 39, 41, 45, 49, 50, 59, 61, 69, 73, 79, 85,
89, 91, 92, 95, 99, 100, 103, 105, 107, 111, 115, 117, 121, 123, 127; Corbis: pp.43, 47, 53,
77, 81, 109; Getty: pp.9, 12, 26, 86, 97; Photolibrary: pp.19, 34, 57, 64, 67, 75, 119.
Jacket picture credits: Front cover: Corbis; Back cover top and middle: Photolibrary;
bottom: Getty.

A CIP catalogue record for this book is available from the British Library.

Printed in Singapore

ARCHITECTURE

The 50 most influential architects in the world

JOHN STONES

CONTENTS

Mid-century Modern

Post-Modern to the Present

INTRODUCTION

Shaping the spaces in which we live, architects play a vital part in all our lives. Great works of architecture have the ability to make our lives better and our spirits soar, while poor designs can lead to isolation and misery.

Ludwig Mies van der Rohe famously stated that 'architecture starts when you carefully put two bricks together'. Yet the results of putting these bricks together have been various. It is a surprisingly small handful of highly original architects who have dramatically affected the built environment in which we find ourselves, whether churches, galleries, office blocks or social housing. This book features a selection of the most significant of these architects, whose achievements vary from the questioning of design processes and materials and the creation of novel forms to the development of radical social theories and the emulation and reinterpretation of past architectural styles.

An appreciation of the minds and innovations of some of the most significant architects can transform a casual stroll through any city or town, as we begin to perceive their influence on the built environment around us. These pioneering architects were often (and continue to be) imbued with an enormous self-belief that enabled them to imprint a new vision of reality on their surroundings, allowing their ideas to become actual physical realities rather than merely designs on a drawing board.

The innovative structures designed by these individual architects have had a profound

'All architecture is shelter, all great architecture is the design of space that contains, cuddles, exalts, or stimulates the persons in that space.'

Philip Johnson

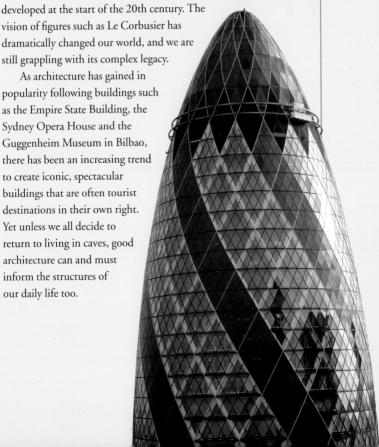

and influential effect on the development of architecture. Architects draw on the work of colleagues past and present, working within and against traditions. Such influence has given rise to two of the most prominent strands in the history of architecture.

First is the Classical, referring to the buildings of Ancient Greece and Rome. They have repeatedly been a source of inspiration for Western architecture century after century, from the Italian Renaissance and Palladio to the Neo-Classicism of the 18th and 19th centuries, and more recently the totalitarian regimes of Nazi Germany and Fascist Italy and the Post-Modernists of the late 20th century.

The second strand is Modernism, which was responsible for a radically new conception of architecture that broke with tradition and developed at the start of the 20th century. The vision of figures such as Le Corbusier has dramatically changed our world, and we are still grappling with its complex legacy.

As architecture has gained in popularity following buildings such as the Empire State Building, the Sydney Opera House and the Guggenheim Museum in Bilbao, there has been an increasing trend to create iconic, spectacular buildings that are often tourist destinations in their own right. Yet unless we all decide to return to living in caves, good architecture can and must inform the structures of our daily life too.

Filippo Brunelleschi

Filippo Brunelleschi is the most important architect of early Renaissance Italy, who began a profound engagement with the architecture of Ancient Rome that would dominate European architecture for centuries. He is particularly known for the dome of the cathedral in Florence.

Born: 1377, Florence, Italy
Importance: Re-awakened interest in the architecture of Ancient Rome for the Italian Renaissance
Died: 1446, Florence, Italy

Sixteenth-century Italian Renaissance chronicler Vasari wrote, 'we can surely say he was sent by heaven to renew the art of architecture', referring to the Florentine architect who was to have such a significant impact on European culture. 'For hundreds of years men had neglected this art and had squandered their wealth on buildings without order, badly executed and poorly designed, which were full of strange inventions, shamefully devoid of grace and execrably ornamented.'

The architectural style inherited by Brunelleschi that is so criticised by Vasari we still know by his pejorative appellation of 'Gothic'. Its fanciful ornate style was still current during his early career, but Brunelleschi was part of an elite group of thinkers and artists intent on rediscovering Ancient Rome, and it was he more than anyone else who introduced this mindset to the world of architecture.

Brunelleschi is believed to have visited Rome to inspect ancient ruins in the company of the sculptor Donatello and studied carefully the architectural theories and drawings of *De Architectura* written by Roman author Vitruvius (who died around 15AD). This allowed him to reintroduce a rational approach to building based on advanced mathematical calculations. It also encouraged him to design structures that were much simpler than had hitherto been fashionable, and he began to use classical orders (Doric, Ionic and Corinthian) correctly according to ancient practice.

The new and clean architectural style was already apparent in his first major architectural commission in 1419, an orphanage known as the Ospedale degli Innocenti (Hospital of the Innocents) in Florence. Its simple lines and subtle symmetry marked a major development.

Brunelleschi lost out in a competition with sculptor Lorenzo Ghilberti to design the doors for the large baptistery in front of Santa Maria del Fiore, the cathedral of Florence. Later, however, a competition was held to find an architect to build a dome over the cathedral. With the support of the mighty Medici family, Brunelleschi won, apparently after making a egg stand on end on a piece of polished marble.

The original design for the church, begun over a century earlier, ambitiously envisaged a dome that at 45m (148ft) across would be larger even than that of the Pantheon in Rome. The technical ability to pull off this feat of engineering was not yet available, however. The Roman Pantheon, for instance, relied on concrete, the recipe for which had been forgotten.

Brunelleschi's solution was an octagonal structure famously made up of more than a million bricks. Work started in 1420 and took 16 years to complete. As well as being a beautiful building of symbolic importance for Florence, it is also an important example of structural engineering. Brunelleschi designed many other churches and sacred structures in Florence, including the radically austere and influential Santo Spirito (1428).

The dome of the cathedral of Florence (Santa Maria del Fiore), Brunelleschi's most famous legacy.

GOTHIC CATHEDRALS

**Between 1140 and 1250 a radically new style of architecture –
the result of collaboration between architects, stone masons
and clerics – emerged that would have impact all over Europe
and characterise the later Middle Ages. Now known as Gothic,
its greatest expression was in the spectacular feats of design
and engineering exhibited in the construction of cathedrals
in France.**

It is commonly accepted that the Gothic style began with the
design of the choir of the Church of St Denis near Paris in 1140.
The names of the master craftsmen, structural engineers, masons
and sculptors who jointly conceived and created it – as is the case
with many later Gothic masterpieces – are unknown to us, but we
do know the project was pushed forward by an ambitious and
powerful cleric, Abbot Suger.

The style was originally known as the French style; the word
Gothic was invented as an insult in the Renaissance to describe its
unclassical 'barbarity', but it is this designation that has stuck. Three
cardinal features distinguished Gothic from the crude, solid
Romanesque style that it gradually supplanted: the pointed arch, the
ribbed vault and the flying buttress. St Denis brought these elements
together in a way that allowed for completely novel architecture. In
conjunction with one another, these structural features allowed the
buildings to seem increasingly light and enabled them to become
taller and taller, to appear to reach towards the heavens in a way that
would be awe inspiring for its congregations.

While used for all manner of buildings, the Gothic style was most
important in the design of cathedrals, which were rebuilt in the area
around Paris – the Ile de France – during the 12th and 13th centuries.
In a dazzling competition of one-upmanship, each city sought to

outdo what had previously been attempted, resulting in structures that often took centuries to complete.

Notre Dame de Laon Cathedral (begun around 1160) is an early example of French Gothic architecture. It is relatively simple compared to the cathedrals of Amiens, Rouen, Notre Dame de Paris, Beauvais and Chartres that followed in the hundred years after St Denis. At 48m (157ft) tall, the nave of the still unfinished

> *'A Gothic church is a petrified religion.'*
> Samuel Taylor Coleridge

cathedral of Beauvais is the highest built, outdoing those of buildings such as the Basilica of St Peter's in Rome and St Paul's Cathedral in London. However Chartres (begun in 1194) is often seen as the greatest and most sophisticated example of the Gothic style.

As the style developed, walls could become delicate filigree, almost disappearing behind the stained glass, such as those in Saint Chapelle in Paris (1248), which exemplifies the phase of extreme decoration, sometimes referred to as *rayonnant*, shared with the cathedral of Rheims (c.1211).

Important examples of Gothic cathedrals built in neighbouring countries include those of Canterbury (1175) in England and Cologne (1248) in Germany. The ratio of height to width of the latter cathedral was more extreme than any other example.

In the later 18th and 19th centuries, there was a Romantic revival of interest in Gothic architecture. This included the Neo-Gothic movement, probably the best-known example of which is the Houses of Parliament in London, designed by Sir Charles Barry in 1835.

Neo-Classical Inaugurator
Andrea Palladio

The Renaissance villas designed by Venetian architect Andrea Palladio inaugurated a Neo-Classical architecture that was widely emulated both in Europe and America. He is often held to be the most influential architect of all time.

Born: 1508, Padua, Italy
Importance: Inspired the Neo-Classical idiom that became known as Palladianism
Died: 1580, Maser, Italy

From an inauspicious start as a stone mason in the city of Padua, close to Venice, Palladio rose through the ranks, largely thanks to the support of an enlightened and wealthy patron, Giangiorgio Trissino, who enabled him to visit Rome to study the remains of ancient buildings. Palladio was born Andrea di Pietro; it was Trissino gave him the name, full of classical allusion, by which he continues to be known today.

Palladio's elegant Villa Capra (1566), Vicenza, was much imitated.

Palladio spent most of his working life in the small town of Vicenza, close to both Padua and Venice, which is the site of his most famous buildings, including the Villa Capra or Villa Rotunda (1566). Typical of the new kind of country residence that was being developed during the 16th century, it is a light and airy structure with loggias to all four sides framed by classical columns that allowed an easy integration of inside and out, incorporating the surrounding landscaping into the design.

The floor plan of the Villa Capra is completely symmetrical, structured around an impressive central circular hall with a heavily frescoed dome inspired by the Pantheon in Rome. It is a building of deceptive simplicity that makes systematic use of the elements of the architecture of Ancient Rome in a way that is both light and elegant. These ideas were set out in detail in an extensive (and widely studied) treatise, *I Quattro Libri dell'Architettura* (*The Four Books of Architecture*), which Palladio published in 1570.

The majority of Palladio's commissions were for villas and palaces for the aristocracy, but he also designed some major churches, including San Giorgio Maggiore and the Redentore in Venice. Palladio's final masterpiece, however, was a design for a theatre. The Teatro Olimpico (Olympic Theatre) in Vicenza has a semi circle of stone seating that was influenced by the arenas of Ancient Rome. Work began in the final year of Palladio's life and was finished by fellow Venetian architect Vincenzo Scamozzi, who created a remarkable permanent *trompe l'oeil* stage.

Palladio's buildings, the villas in particular, were always held in high repute and his style was disseminated throughout Europe by wealthy visitors conducting a Grand Tour. They contributed to an architectural style that has become known as Palladianism, which flourished in the 18th century, and whose influence can also be seen in the plantation houses of America's Deep South, the White House in Washington DC and even in modern suburban housing developments.

NEO-CLASSICISM
This term describes the various cultural engagements with the legacy of Ancient Greece and Rome, but is particularly common as a description of the 18th-century craze to create classically influenced architecture and art in Europe and the United States.

Inigo Jones

The first famous English architect, Inigo Jones introduced the Palladian style to British architecture bringing it back into step with mainland Europe. His delicate and refined buildings mark the beginning of a long tradition of Neo-Classicism in Britain.

Born: 1573, London, England
Importance: Introduced classical architecture to Britain
Died: 1652, London, England

Inigo Jones was born in London to a humble Catholic family of cloth makers. He first worked as a set and costume designer on the extensive and elaborate courtly entertainments or masques, and learnt architecture through building the sophisticated structures these productions required rather than through any formal training. The work also brought Jones into contact with aristocrats, who began to commission buildings from him and supported his journeys abroad.

Jones visited Italy twice and made particular study of Palladio's works, reading and heavily annotating his famous treatise, the *Quattro Libri*. On return from his second visit to Italy in 1615, he was promoted to the influential post of Surveyor-General to the Office of Works, overseeing the royal residences and other courtly buildings. In this role he was heavily involved in early plans to rebuild St Paul's Cathedral, and in his work to develop Covent Garden, he introduced the Italian idea of a piazza or square to Britain.

His first major commission, however, was to design a new residence in Greenwich for Queen Anne of Denmark, wife of James I. This simple, restrained structure was heavily influenced by Italian practice, and its clean, white stucco exterior would have seemed revolutionary set against London's red brick or timbered buildings.

In 1619, construction began on Banqueting House, replacing a structure than had burnt down. This was part of a wider plan to

The Queen's House, Greenwich, was heavily influenced by Jones's travels in Italy.

redevelop the Palace of Whitehall that never took place. Banqueting House was intended as a large public building that could function as a place for masques and other grand ceremonial entertainments staged for James I and his son Charles I. Its form is borrowed from the Roman basilica and the influence of Jones's background as a set designer resulted in his creation of a suitably dramatic space.

The building is also noted for its painted ceiling, depicting *The Apotheosis of James I* by Rubens, then the most famous painter in Europe. This was a considerable coup for Charles I, who was determined to bring the cultural sophistication of mainland Europe to his provincial country. Jones's Palladian building, with its sophisticated façade, was the perfect home for it. Both ceiling and building, however, epitomised the extravagant, foreign-influenced reign that was deeply unpopular with his subjects, and in 1649, Charles I was executed on a scaffold placed in front of Banqueting House.

Jones continues to be noted in architectural history as much for his subsequent influence as for the inherent qualities of his buildings. His designs broke with the outdated Tudor architectural practices that still prevailed in England, introducing contemporary Italianate ideas and set the stage for a future tendency towards Neo-Classicism in England.

Gianlorenzo Bernini

Gianlorenzo Bernini was the pre-eminent figure of the Italian Baroque. Equally at home in painting, sculpture and architecture, his revolutionary, theatrical creations ushered in a radically new approach to public space, and were admired and imitated across Europe.

Born: 1598, Naples, Italy
Importance: Foremost sculptor and architect of the Italian Baroque
Died: 1680, Rome, Italy

Born to a sculptor in Naples, Bernini became one of the most important creative figures in the papal city of Rome. He broke with the previous reverence of ancient models to create confident and exuberant structures, and contributed to the creation of a new style now known as Baroque.

Bernini's enduring contribution to architecture is to have understood its sculptural elements. His synthetic approach to an array of commissions, from fountains to chapels, merged what had been seen as the separate spheres of sculpture and architecture; a sculpture of a saint in a side chapel could be placed with an architectural sensibility while a structure such as a fountain could be made as voluptuous as any work of sculpture.

This approach was already apparent in his first major commission, the Baldacchino for the papal Basilica of St Peter's. It is a canopy over the main altar of the largest and most famous church in the world, supported by outrageously decorated, 20m (66ft) high, copper columns. Experience in stage design allowed Bernini to consider the design in experiential terms and to take light and context into account.

'It is common knowledge that he was the first who undertook to unite architecture, sculpture and painting in a such a way that they make a beautiful whole.'

Filippo Baldinucci

The Piazza of St Peter's, Rome, is revered as Bernini's supreme masterpiece.

The Baldacchino made manifest the potential of gesture in architecture, something that Bernini was to exploit to its full in the Piazza and Colonnade of St Peter's. The enormous oval Piazza is contained by huge semi circular colonnades that reach out like embracing arms from the façade.

Bernini's flexible approach to architectural geometry (developed in tandem with his contemporary, Franscesco Borromini) is also exemplified in S Andrea al Quirinale in Rome (1658-70), which has a curved façade sitting in front of an oval interior space that is wider than it is long. Bernini considered this his most perfect work, but today, other than the Piazza of St Peter's, it is generally his *St Teresa in Ecstasy* (1647), in the Cornaro chapel of the church of Santa Maria della Vittoria in Rome, that is most rated. The highly charged statue of the saint is situated in a marble, faux-architectural setting, dramatically lit by a shaft of natural light in a way that impressively merges all the creative disciplines.

The theatrical works of Bernini and Borromini set the foundation for a fluid architectural style that would last across Europe – particularly in Catholic countries – for more than a century, and is again becoming increasing relevant for contemporary architects.

Christopher Wren

Sir Christopher Wren lived to the grand age of 90, enjoying a long career that has made him the most revered British architect. He heavily influenced the fabric of London as it was rebuilt after the Great Fire of 1666 and is most known for the Neo-Classical St Paul's Cathedral in London.

Born: 1632, East Knoyle, Wiltshire, England
Importance: Designer of St Paul's Cathedral and Britain's most famous architect
Died: 1723, London, England

Wren initially showed brilliance as a scholar at Wadham College in Oxford, reading widely in the sciences, mathematics and classics. He gained particular respect for his experiments and research into astronomy, for which he gained his first professorship at the age of 25.

Wren added architecture to his wide-ranging accomplishments, while continuing his academic career in the sciences. His first building was a chapel for Pembroke College, the first classical structure to join the medieval buildings that made up Oxford University. This chapel was followed by a commission in 1663 for the Sheldonian Theatre, also in Oxford. With an elegant yet imposing curved Neo-Classical façade, it is now one of the landmarks of the university town.

In 1666, the Great Fire swept through the capital, destroying 80 per cent of homes, churches and civic buildings. Seeing an opportunity in the catastrophe, Wren submitted ambitious designs to Charles II that proposed a complete and radical remodelling of London, with grandly laid out avenues replacing cramped medieval streets.

While these were not implemented, they did result in Wren's appointment in 1669 as Surveyor General to the King's Works, with a special remit to

'Geometrical figures are naturally more beautiful than any irregular.'

rebuild more than 50 churches, including the old cathedral of St Paul's. He also designed the still extant Monument to the disaster, a 62m (203ft) Doric column, close to the site near London Bridge where the fire started.

So iconic has the shape of St Paul's become that it is hard to understand the break the building made with its predecessors and other churches in Britain. It took a great leap of faith and many revisions before the commissioning committee could finally accept that an Italianate building, featuring elements from Pagan Ancient Rome, should be used for the most important ecclesiastical building of the Church of England. Imposing and impressive, St Paul's is also a building of great refinement and delicacy.

As well as the many inventive and elegant churches that he either designed or oversaw, Wren also designed the Royal Observatory in Greenwich; fitting, given his earlier career as an astronomer. One of his final projects was Greenwich Hospital, now known as the Old Royal Naval Chapel. Situated on the banks of the Thames, its two component buildings frame the view to an earlier pioneer in British classicism – the Queen's House designed by Inigo Jones.

If Jones introduced Neo-Classicism to England, Wren developed it into an original, inventive and yet restrained language that would typify British architecture and distinguish it from the flamboyant exuberance of the Baroque and Rococo buildings of mainland Europe.

Some 300 years after its completion, St Paul's Cathedral remains one of London's most visited sites.

Robert Adam

Last in the triumvirate of great British Classicist architects that includes Inigo Jones and Christopher Wren, Robert Adam was less concerned with grand statements than with developing highly sophisticated, themed interior decorations. His work was so popular that it gave rise to what has become known as 'Adam Style'.

Born: 1728, Kirkcaldy, Fife, Scotland

Importance: Proponent of a sophisticated form of Neo-Classicism particularly influential for interior design

Died: 1792, London, England

Born in Scotland to an architect father, Adam learnt his skills on joining the successful family practice in Edinburgh. At the age of 26, he set off on the Grand Tour of Europe, with Italy as the highlight. In Rome, he encountered the passionate researches of German art historian Johann Joachim Winckelmann, who was responding to the recent excavation of Pompeii and Herculaneum. There he also became deeply impressed by Piranesi's atmospheric and eccentric engravings of antiquities and studied with him for a while.

On his return to Britain four years later, Adam's work began to distill these influences into a new eclectic and sophisticated kind of Classicism. While the Palladians looked principally to Ancient Rome for inspiration, and felt the need to adhere to abstract rules derived from the treatises of Vitruvius and Palladio, Robert Adam was able to draw on his travels, considerable erudition and many other influences, including Greek, Byzantine and Baroque, in his decorative schemes, which often followed a set theme. For instance, motifs from the vases of the ancient Etruscans were used to design the 'Etruscan' room for the stately home of Osterley Park (1761).

The wealthy embraced this new style, and Adam, now in practice in London with his brother James, was in great demand. The brothers were commissioned to design, build or decorate fashionable homes, often supervising projects closely and sometimes acting as speculative developers themselves.

Unusually, the interiors of their buildings were accorded the same attention as the exterior, and the brothers were usually responsible for the actual decoration and furniture, often designing it themselves. Home House, in London designed by Robert Adam in 1777, is a typical example. A grand London residence taken over from a previous architect, it saves its best for inside, in particular a spectacular yet very delicate cantilevered circular staircase under a glass dome.

In 1770, the brothers began work on Pulteney Bridge in Bath. It is a stone bridge lined with shops, clearly

The imposing cantilevered circular staircase of Home House, London.

influenced by the Ponte Vecchio in Florence and the Ponte di Rialto in Venice (both of which Robert would have visited) but executed with restraint and British understatement.

Like the more formal Palladian style, Robert Adam's work was much emulated in the US, where it became known as the Federal style for patriotic reasons after the War of Independence. Another element of his legacy was the importance he placed on interior design, which had not previously been, nor was always subsequently, accorded the same status as the design of buildings. But he also pioneered a blend of architecture and fashion that remains controversial today.

CLASSICAL ARCHITECTURE

The buildings of Ancient Greece and Rome have exerted an enduring influence on the architecture of the West. As with law, philosophy, medicine and literature, Europeans and Americans have tended, sometimes erroneously and over selectively, to see their origins in these two related ancient civilisations. As the appellation 'classical' would suggest, the way in which the architecture of Ancient Greece and Rome is understood and appreciated has a heavy retrospective slant.

While ancient Greece produced a variety of buildings, it is primarily the temple architecture of the Periklean period that is seen as exemplary, in particular the Parthenon. Situated on the Acropolis and dominating Athens, the Parthenon is a Doric temple to the goddess and protector Athena. Perikles bgan its construction in 447BC after the sacking of Athens by the Persians. With its open Doric colonnades and triangular pediment, it remains one of the most recognisable of all buildings, inspiring imitation in later centuries in anything from grand civic buildings and museums to decorative elements in suburban housing.

However it was only in the 18th century that an archaeological awareness of sufficient sophistication developed to allow a clear separation to be made between the art and architecture of Ancient Greece and the later art and architecture of Ancient Rome. Thanks to the research of pioneering figures such as Johann Joachim Winckelmann, a German historian resident in Rome, a new and enthusiastic understanding of the Ancient Greek world was developed. These researches underpinned a Hellenism, in contrast to a generalised Classicism, that was to be particularly important in Germany and the US, where the aesthetic attributes of Greek architecture also signalled democratic aspirations and virtues.

Previously, the understanding of ancient architecture was derived primarily from Rome and its many ruins. Following the pioneering re-evaluation of these ruins by early Renaissance figures such as Filippo Brunelleschi, these became the almost obligatory objects of study for artists and architects.

The buildings of the Forum attested to the refined civic architecture of the Romans, while the impressive Colosseum amphitheatre (begun around 70AD) also demonstrated the engineering prowess of the Romans. However, one building in particular stood out – the Pantheon. This temple was built in the second century AD, with a massive dome some 43m (141ft) across constructed using concrete of various densities. The dramatic central circular space is accompanied by a small rectilinear portico.

Thanks to Roman engineer and architect Marcus Vitruvius Pollio (who is believed to have lived from 75BC to about 15AD), much of the knowledge and rules of ancient architecture survives. Vitruvius (as he is usually known) published *De Architectura* (*The Ten Books on Architecture*), which was widely read during the Renaissance and after, and which set out, among other issues, the correct uses (and fanciful origins) of the three so-called orders – Doric, Ionic and Corinthian – that were derived from Greek precedent.

> 'The one way for us to become great, perhaps inimitable, is by imitating the ancients.'
>
> Johann Joachim Winckelmann

While only a handful of buildings were to exert influence on subsequent architecture, the detailed study of Ancient Greek and Roman architecture of all periods yields a much fuller and more complex picture of what the architecture of the ancient world actually encompassed.

Karl Friedrich Schinkel

Germany's greatest Neo-Classical architect, the Prussian Karl Friedrich Schinkel had a profound impact on the rebuilding of Berlin after the Napoleonic Wars. His prolific and varied career has inspired many different forms of architecture.

Born: 1781, near Berlin, Germany
Importance: Reshaped the architecture of Berlin in various historicist styles
Died: 1841, Berlin, Germany

Born into a family of Lutheran pastors, Schinkel studied architecture with the father and son Friedrich and David Gilly, both ardent Neo-Classicists. He worked first as a stage designer before moving into architecture, where he combined the Romantic imagination of a painter with a practical and logical approach to planning.

Appointed Surveyor to the Prussian Building Commission in 1815, after the defeat of the Napoleonic forces, Schinkel set about creating buildings that would reflect Berlin's new status as a European superpower, re-inventing the way cities were planned (a concept we now call urban planning). While some of his more ambitious ideas remained on the drawing board, many were built.

Buildings such as the Neue Wache (New Watch) of 1816 and the Konzerthaus Berlin (Concert Hall) of 1818 exemplified a new, more subtle and mature, Classicism. Palladian-inspired architecture had principally looked to the achievements of Ancient Rome. However, German Classicists, following the works of Johann Winckelmann, aligned themselves with Ancient Greece and sought a rebirth of Germany in its spirit (rather than that of Ancient Rome, which was associated with the Romance nations, in particular the enemy, France). Perhaps Schinkel's most famous work in this idiom is the Altes Museum (1822) in Berlin, inspired by Greek Doric temple design.

Advancements in German archaeology and scholarship also allowed other, previously sidelined, styles to be studied. On his visits to Italy, Schinkel was as interested in Medieval, Gothic and Islamic structures as the hallowed greats of Rome. As well as the Neo-Greek architecture for which he is best known, he also pioneered the Neo-Gothic style, evident in the Kreuzberg War Memorial (1818–21), topped with an iron cross, which has become famous as the emblem of Prussia. The Friedrichswerdersche Kirche (1824–30) pioneered a Neo-Gothic approach to church design that was also highly influential.

The Bauakademie (School of Architecture), built in Berlin (1831–34), was a red-brick structure noteworthy for its utilitarian design and lack of ornament, anticipating later architectural developments. Unfortunately the building was heavily bombed during World War II and later destroyed, but plans are afoot to rebuild it.

The rich diversity of Schinkel's architecture has been an important point of reference for architects of diametrically opposed positions. His eclectic appropriation of different architectural styles set a precedent for Post-Modernists, while pioneering Modernists such as Adolf Loos and Ludwig Mies van der Rohe admired his logical, technological approach and restrained ornamentation. His grand designs prepared the ground for the modern discipline of urban planning while inspiring schemes dreamt up by Hitler and his architect Albert Speer.

The Altes Museum (1822), Berlin, probably Schinkel's most important work, created a much-emulated template for museum design both in Germany and abroad.

Georges-Eugène Haussmann

Baron Georges-Eugène Haussmann's grand civic scheme transformed Paris, modernising it into the elegant and rational city we know today. Hugely ambitious, it saw large parts of the French capital destroyed to create grand boulevards, open public spaces structured around monuments and a logical, systematic road layout.

Born: 1809, Paris, France
Importance: Highly influential urban planner and creator of modern Paris
Died: 1891, Paris, France

While Paris had long been the pre-eminent city of Europe, it was also famed for its unsanitary and crowded medieval streets and slums, leading to traffic congestion and repeated outbreaks of diseases such as cholera. On election as President of the Republic, Louis-Napoléon Bonaparte (Napoléon III) set about modernising the economy and fabric of the battered country, including the capital Paris. This enormous undertaking was entrusted to Georges-Eugène

Wide boulevards characterised Haussmann's scheme for the French capital.

Haussmann, not an architect but a civil servant from a Protestant family, whose German name pointed to origins in the Alsace area. Appointed Prefect of the Seine in 1852, Haussmann conceived and oversaw the enormous project, previously unparalleled in scope.

Central Paris was completely redesigned, starting with a cartographic blueprint that would impose a rational, geometric form to its streets and require the destruction of most of medieval Paris. Wide tree-lined boulevards connected the newly constructed train stations, opera houses and national monuments, such as the Arc de Triomphe. These boulevards were bordered by new apartment buildings, whose overall height and many other dimensions were set by law, creating a cohesive aesthetic effect. The width of boulevards was also partly dictated by engineering considerations, such as the new sewage and public transport systems that were at the heart of the modernisation of the city. They also functioned as a means of social control, creating wide open spaces where the populace could be more easily controlled by military policing methods.

Haussmann's schemes encountered vigorous opposition on many fronts, including the exorbitant cost of the project (totalling many hundreds of millions of francs), some 20 years of major building works that nearly paralysed the city and a resulting change in the social mix, with the poor being effectively forced out of the new centre by the higher rents charged in the new buildings. So unpopular did Haussmann become that he was eventually fired in 1870.

But his design of modern Paris continues to be one of the most influential and wide-ranging examples of urban planning, emulated by later urban planners who worked to modernise major cities such as Vienna, Chicago, Barcelona and London. Many of his ideas about traffic organisation, the role of parks, building height restrictions and public transport are taken for granted today, and the profile of urban planning was raised immeasurably for good. The term 'Haussmannism' has gained currency, but has two sides, as his name is also associated with the alienation of modern urban life and insensitive bureaucratic schemes that ignore the will of the people.

THE INDUSTRIAL REVOLUTION AND IRON STRUCTURES

By the middle of the 19th century, architecture had largely split into two separate practices. There were the elaborate, ornate historicist buildings, often with masonry facades, designed by esteemed architects, and then there were the anonymous structures, usually for commercial purposes, such factories, built as part of the process of industrialisation and mechanisation. The irony is that it was these latter buildings, whose design was often carried out by engineers or tradesmen, that were the more innovative and that would fuel subsequent innovations in architecture.

The material typically used for these commercial structures was iron. Previously neglected as a building material, iron could now be mass produced. It became one of the building blocks of the Industrial Revolution, allowing the creation of railways, factories and suspension bridges that would transform societies. For designers of arcades, greenhouses and railway stations, the use of iron and glass offered novel and attractive structural possibilities.

The greenhouse or conservatory, in particular, became immensely popular, and a chance for virtuoso displays of these new technologies. The most famous is example is the Crystal Palace, an enormous 564m (1,850ft) long steel and glass structure erected in Hyde Park for the 1851 Great Exhibition in London, staged to wow the world with Britain's industrial prowess. The Crystal Palace featured a remarkably prescient modular construction that allowed prefabrication and easy disassembly. Tellingly, its designer, Joseph Paxton (1803–65), was not an architect but a gardener by training.

As well as showcasing the potential of these new construction methods, the Crystal Palace also demonstrated the considerable propaganda benefit of both a world exhibition and spectacular architectural feature. A variety of such events were held in following decades in major cities such as Paris and Chicago, and these often acted as a spur to the development of new technologies and impressive structural feats.

'All that is solid melts into air, all that is holy is profaned, and man is at last compelled to face with sober senses, his real conditions of life, and his relations with his kind.'

Karl Marx

One of the people involved was French engineer Gustav Eiffel, who had also devised groundbreaking and daring iron bridges. For the 1889 Paris exhibition, the lessons learnt in the design and construction of these bridges were put to a new purpose – a steel observation tower some 300m (984ft) high, set upon four gigantic girders. Dominating Paris, the tower was seen initially as an ugly image of modernity, before gradually becoming one of the world's best-known and most-loved buildings. The Eiffel Tower remained the world's tallest structure until the erection of the Chrysler building in New York in 1930.

While the chasm between structural engineering and architecture continued to grow, the use of iron (and steel after 1860) and glass alerted future architects to novel structural possibilities and treatments. The large-scale use of glass – and increased sophistication of its manufacture – was particularly important for the early European Modernists, while the innovatory use of structural steel in the US made possible the erection of the high-rises and skyscrapers that would define modernity.

Charles Francis Annesley Voysey

An important designer and architect of the Arts and Crafts movement, Charles Voysey translated its ideals into architectural forms to create an enduring domestic vernacular language that has proved particularly influential for suburban housing.

Born: 1857, Hessle, Yorkshire, England
Importance: Creator of an Arts and Crafts vernacular style widely emulated in suburban housing
Died: 1941, Winchester, England

The Arts and Crafts movement was premised on the utopian idea that aesthetics, in particular a return to craft and handiwork, could heal the desolation and social violence brought about by the ravages of the Industrial Revolution. Inspired by Romanticism, and the art critic John Ruskin in particular, Arts and Crafts practitioners looked back to an idealised past of country cottages inhabited by self-sufficient craftspeople.

The movement's high priest was William Morris, whose interests ranged from poetry to wallpaper and who had a devoted following, but in architecture its most important exponent was the diminutive Yorkshireman Charles Francis Annesley Voysey. Voysey worked with a variety of architects in London before establishing his own practice in 1883. While awaiting commissions, he, like William Morris, began designing wallpapers with repeating patterns, which proved very popular and which he carried on creating for a variety of manufacturers throughout his career. Soon, however, he was in much demand as a designer of country houses, ironically often for the wealthy, who appreciated the easy charm of his buildings and their effortless and subtle referencing of the poetic medieval and Tudor heritage.

Two features, in particular, typify the town and country homes he designed. First are the distinctive heavily pitched roofs, which suggested the thatched cottages in a previous age but were translated

Though large, Broad Leys, Cumbria, is typically sensitive and self-effacing.

into contemporary terms and executed with modern technology. These were often so heavily pitched that the windows of the top story are set into the roofs of the buildings, creating a dreamy effect. White-painted pebble-dashing often evoked the lime-washed medieval house. Second are the long horizontal ribbon windows, which maximised interior light while making the most of views. Like the simple unfussy forms of the many pieces of furniture he designed, they anticipated later Modernist designs.

In 1900, Voysey designed and built himself an influential house in a suburb of North London. The Orchard, as he called it, was executed on a small scale to suit his short height, and Voysey carefully designed every element from the building to the furniture and wallpaper. Built in 1898 and on a much larger scale overlooking Lake Windermere in the north of England, the stately home of Broad Leys is another of his masterpieces.

Voysey's development of a new domestic vernacular, of houses with period detail created for comfortable living, found wide resonance and was replicated in suburban developments around the world. Many who copied his designs, however, did so with only a very superficial understanding of his work, resulting in suburbs full of timbered homes soon to be derided as 'Mock Tudor'.

GARDEN SUBURBS

The garden city suburbs of early 20th-century England, harking back to a country idyll of centuries past, present a powerful antidote to the Modernist architecture and monumental buildings that dominate the architectural history of the 20th century. Focusing on aspects such as quality of life and access to gardens and open spaces, the garden cities were imitated by town planners and property developers around the world.

The impact of the Industrial Revolution was felt with more violence in Britain than in any other European country, resulting in a large urban poor population living in squalid slums. The manifest injustices fuelled the emergence of many different kinds of socialism across Europe, including a utopian variety that was very British and informed the practices of the Arts and Crafts Movement and its leader William Morris. Looking to a pastoral 'never-never land', they envisaged designing an environment that could bring a fractured society back together.

These ideas were applied to town planning by Ebenezer Howard (1850–1928), an urban theorist who, in 1898, published *To-Morrow: A Peaceful Path to Real Reform.* It was an enormously influential book, which is still studied today by town planners, and the impact of its teachings can be felt by anyone visiting a suburb. Soon reprinted as *Garden Cities of To-Morrow,* the book set out in great detail Howard's alternative vision of a Garden City. This would be a self-sufficient conurbation of around 32,000 people and mix the benefits of town and country. Its master plan as well as its detail would be designed for the health of its citizens. Howard conceived the now common idea of 'zoning', separating the different activities and functions by areas, which were presented in a concentric scheme, radiating from a central square. This would be surrounded by a 'green belt', an idea that was subsequently applied to cities around the world, most famously to the planning of London.

Founded in 1903 and not far from London, Letchworth Garden City was the first to put Howard's ideas into action. Designed by Barry Parker and Raymond Unwin, the new city was admired and ridiculed in equal measure. It initially appealed to non-conformists such as vegetarians and Quakers, and the public consumption of alcohol was banned in Letchworth until after World War II.

Executed on a smaller scale and founded in 1907 in North London, Hampstead Garden Suburb is the most well-known example of the garden city. Its central square and two churches were designed by Sir Edwin Lutyens, and the residential housing was executed in a mix of Neo-Georgian and Voysey-inspired idioms that continues to be replicated in suburban housing around the world, from Russia to Australia – and to be despised by the majority of serious architects.

> '*Nothing short of the discovery of a method for constructing magnets of yet greater power than our cities possess can be effective for redistributing the population in a spontaneous and healthy manner.*'
>
> Ebenezer Howard

Yet as Modernism's central tenets came to be questioned in the final decades of the 20th century, and the grand housing schemes inspired by the ideals of its leading figures fell into disrepute, seen as dens of alienation, fear and crime, the previously derided model of the garden suburb began again to be investigated by architects, urban planners and local governments interested in finding a solution to providing housing schemes that would be popular with their residents.

Greene and Greene

Greene and Greene developed a new approach to domestic architecture that was to be widely emulated, particularly in their home state of California. Their seminal bungalows, created in the first two decades of the 20th century, took elements from Japanese architecture to create spacious new open-plan homes that were designed for easy living.

Born: (Charles Sumner Greene) 1868, Cincinnati, Ohio, United States; (Henry Mather Greene) 1870, Cincinnati, Ohio, United States
Importance: Developed the informal and luxurious modern Californian bungalow
Died: (Charles) 1957, Carmel-by-the-Sea, California, United States; (Henry) 1954, Pasadena, California, United States

The two brothers Charles Sumner Greene and Henry Mather Greene both enrolled to study architecture at Massachusetts Institute of Technology in Boston at the same time, but then practised separately with different leading Boston architects.

In 1893, en route to join their parents, who had moved to the then small Californian town of Pasadena, the brothers encountered the architecture of Japan at the Chicago World Fair. It was to prove a decisive moment in their design philosophy. A year later, they set up their own joint practice as Greene and Greene, designing a variety of buildings, including the domestic houses for which they would become renowned.

Gamble House, the most famous of Greene and Greene's 'bungalows', was built in 1909.

Their bungalows were luxurious conceptions that took their location and the Californian climate very much into consideration, involving a free interplay with the outside and featuring open, breezy layouts. The most famous was Gamble House, built in 1909 for a scion of the Gamble family that had made its fortune with the consumer goods company Proctor and Gamble. Their client was typical of a new Californian generation of millionaires looking to establish their own identity and style.

Despite its usual classification as a bungalow, Gamble is a large structure over three stories. It creates an informal relationship with the outside through the use of extensive balconies, porches and eaves constructed from redwood, and the design shows an indebtedness to traditional Japanese temple architecture. The mahogany panelled inside was as finely detailed as the outside.

Like their Arts and Crafts and Art Nouveau contemporaries in Europe, the brothers conceived their houses as total designs, often working on every detail of the interiors too, creating bespoke furniture and fittings, sometimes even the cutlery, textiles and picture frames as well as stained glass. This entailed the brothers spending considerable time on site, and often led to unpopular delays in construction that ultimately would count against them. In 1922, Charles moved to Carmel-by-the-Sea and the practice was dissolved. While there was no animosity and both brothers continued to practice separately as architects, the days of their greatest achievements were over.

The open-plan bungalows designed by Greene and Greene in their heyday created a very influential modern idiom for Californian residential architecture. Their designs decisively changed American architecture, showing the way to a distinctive language that combined the modern, informal and luxurious in a novel fashion.

ART NOUVEAU
Characterised by its elegant and voluptuous organic curves, Art Nouveau is a decorative style that became prominent across Europe at the end of the 19th century. Literally it means 'new style' and is used interchangeably with the terms Jugendstil in German and Stile Liberty or Liberty style in Italian.

Victor Horta

Belgian architect Baron Victor Horta was the most famous proponent of the Art Nouveau style that dominated European design at the turn of the century and is usually credited with introducing its characteristic language to the practice of architecture.

Born: 1861, Ghent, Belgium
Importance: First to apply Art Nouveau style to architecture
Died: 1947, Brussels, Belgium

The son of a shoemaker in the provincial city of Ghent, where he studied architecture, Horta escaped to Paris, where he worked as an interior designer, enthusiastically imbibing the atmosphere of the French capital and keeping abreast of the artist developments taking place there. On the death of his father, he returned to Belgium and resumed his study of architecture at the Académie Royale des Beaux-Arts.

One of the first major projects he worked on, with his teacher Alphonse Balat, architect to the King of Belgium, was a complex of greenhouses for the Gardens of Laeken. These highly ornate glass palaces allowed him to develop an appreciation of the structural and decorative uses of steel, something that would characterise many of his later buildings.

In 1893, Horta designed the Hotel Tassel, seen as the first major expression of Art Nouveau in architecture. This large town house in Brussels has a stone-clad façade that integrates rich decoration and structural features in an entirely novel way. Extensive use of steel and glass allows a hitherto unimagined lightness for a domestic building.

His early career as an interior designer gave Horta an unusually sensitive appreciation of interior light and space, as well as a totalising concept of design, in which every element participated in the same aesthetic to create a coherent experience. The materials used, which included glass and mosaic, lent these spaces a special and exotic flavour.

Horta put Art Nouveau's botanical shapes and extravagant arabesques to use in his designs in an integrated way rather than as mere decoration. His organic staircases with their wrought-iron railings, often under decorated glass atriums, are especially admired for their grace and beauty. These features are apparent in the house he built for himself in 1898, the Horta House. Its preserved interior is seen as one of the fullest expressions of Art Nouveau.

Art Nouveau rapidly fell from grace as the functional aesthetic of the Modernists, who dismissed his designs as superficial decoration, grew in prominence. However, Horta continued to practice, creating buildings such as the Central Station in Brussels (inaugurated in 1952) that were indebted to Art Nouveau's innovations.

A measure of the extent of the disrepute into which Art Nouveau fell is the destruction of many of his key buildings, which are now known only from photographs. However, historians today see his work as an important bridge between the architecture of the 19th century and the Modernists of the 20th century. The 'psychedelic' 1960s saw a renewed interest in Art Nouveau and Horta's oeuvre, which became highly fashionable again in the 1970s.

Horta House, built by Horta for himself in 1898, is now the Musée Horta.

Henri van de Velde

Belgian architect Henri van de Velde was an important exponent of the Art Nouveau style, developing its functional aspects in a way that would lay the foundations for the Modernism of succeeding generations. A committed pedagogue , he exerted a considerable influence on the architecture of his time.

Born: 1863, Antwerp, Belgium
Importance: Transitional architect who developed the functional aspects of Art Nouveau
Died: 1957, Oberägeri, Switzerland

Van de Velde started off as a painter, before, like his compatriot Victor Horta, moving into interior design. Like Horta, he created highly aestheticised environments during the early part of his career, paying meticulous attention to detail with bespoke furniture and decorative features, which marked the high point of Art Nouveau. But van de Velde also shared the utopian beliefs of the Arts and Crafts movement and his progressive Austrian contemporaries in the transformative abilities of art and architecture.

Van de Velde's first building, the Bloemenwerf House (1895), built as a home for himself in a suburb of Brussels, caused a sensation with its bold forms and decorative timbering. Yet van de Velde is important in architectural history as much for his teaching and writing as for his buildings. Much of his career was spent in Germany, where in 1905 he was invited to become the director of the new Grand Ducal School of Arts and Crafts in Weimar. He also designed its building (1907), a forthright, heavily glassed structure that made a feature of the functional qualities of the materials used in its construction. His Werkbund Theatre (1914), an early foray into reinforced concrete, extended this aspect of his work, and influenced the designs of German Expressionist architect Erich Mendelsohn.

During World War I his Belgian nationality became problematic and van de Velde was succeeded by his protégé Walter Gropius. In

1919 Gropius merged this institution with the Weimar Academy of Fine Arts to create the Bauhaus, the most important engine of Modernist architecture in the 20th century.

His final building was the Boekentoren, or Book Tower, which houses the library of the University of Ghent, where van de Velde spend the latter part of his career as a professor of architecture. It's an austere 64m (210ft) structure situated at the city's high point and has become one of its most recognisable landmarks.

In the debates that raged at the start of the 20th century, van de Velde took a stance that would divide him from the generation of architects that succeeded him. Technology, van de Velde argued, should be in the service of craft; for Walter Gropius and the Modernists, technology was to become an end in itself. But while ultimately he was left behind, van de Velde remains a pivotal figure in the transformation of architecture into the Modernism that would so dominate the 20th century.

The Weimar School of Arts and Crafts (1907).

Charles Rennie Mackintosh

Scottish architect Charles Rennie Mackintosh developed a strikingly original style that mixed the organic decorative forms of Art Nouveau and the idioms of Japanese design. This new, instantly recognisable, stylistic language was applied as a total design that would encompass buildings as well as their furnishings, colours, cutlery and even typography.

Born: 1868, Glasgow, Scotland
Importance: Combined Art Nouveau and Japanese influences to create a distinctive style
Died: 1928, London, England

Mackintosh was born in Glasgow, where he spent most of his life. Apprenticed to architects, he slowly worked his way up to become a partner at Honeyman & Keppie, while keeping abreast of the most progressive developments in European design, art and architecture and entering international competitions.

His principal influences were the Art Nouveau and Beaux Arts styles that had swept through Europe, but to this he added something new – elements drawn from Japan. The ending of Japanese isolation in 1844 and the gradual resumption of trade with the outside world allowed European artists and designers to encounter an entirely new aesthetic. While painters such as van Gogh were heavily influenced by Japanese woodprints, Mackintosh was inspired by the simple elegance and restraint of traditional Japanese furniture and room design. His interiors used screens and subtle light effects rather than the ornate embellishments often expected. Colours were strictly controlled, most notably in the supremely accomplished interiors for Hill House (1903), a home he designed near Glasgow, whose rooms are predominantly white, with delicate decorative touches.

'Construction should be decorated, and not decoration constructed.'

The Willow Tea Rooms (1896) in Glasgow exemplify his unified approach to design – everything, from the building down to the chairs, menus and uniforms, was designed by Mackintosh with the collaboration of his wife Margaret Macdonald.

The interior of Willow Tea Rooms (1896), Glasgow, commissioned by one of Mackintosh's loyal patrons.

The Glasgow School of Art, built in stages between 1899 and 1909, was Mackintosh's first major commission and also his masterpiece. Like the Arts and Crafts Movement, with which he shared many interests, architectural heritage became an important factor. Rather than the Tudor that inspired his English contemporaries, such as Voysey, Mackintosh looked to the 'Celtic' forms of Baronial Scotland, such as heavy masonry. The rhythmical, austere façade of the Glasgow School of Art was constructed out of heavy stone, broken by enormous windows with wrought-ironwork decoration. With the design of its highly detailed interior, Macintosh was suddenly a star for progressive architects across Europe.

Mackintosh's reputation spread quickly, and he was particularly feted by Austrian architects, who saw in him a kindred spirit and invited him to show at the Vienna Secession. At home, however, his innovative style brought him little in the way of success or major commissions outside of Glasgow, and his last years were spent painting watercolours, both architectural and landscape. While Mackintosh's striking originality makes him something of an anomaly, his works were important for designers seeking to forge a new path after Art Nouveau, and he has become immensely popular, particularly for his furniture designs and typography.

Otto Wagner

Otto Wagner was an important Austrian architect, theorist and urban planner who worked in a variety of styles. He was father to a generation of architects in Vienna, sometimes referred to as the Wagner School, who were to be highly influential internationally. His work, in particular, is noted for his architectural realism, or functional use of materials.

Born: 1841, Vienna, Austria
Importance: Developed an architectural realism that anticipated Modernism
Died: 1918, Vienna, Austria

Unlike many famous architects, Wagner presided over a successful and large practice in Vienna, his home city and capital of the Austro-Hungarian Empire. Initially, the structures he designed were of a generic historicist nature, but he was open to influences that allowed him to develop a much more original architecture.

Wagner was a transitional figure, and while many of his buildings seem ornamental and full of period charm to us today, they were often perceived as radical and difficult by his contemporaries. He believed in developing new construction methods suited to the new materials available, and many of his buildings place an emphasis on function that anticipated the 'form follows function' mantra of later Modernists. This is apparent in his undisputed masterpiece, the Österreichische Postsparkasse, or Austrian Post Office Savings Bank, built in stages between 1904 and 1912. 'Nowhere has the slightest sacrifice been made for the benefit of any traditional form', wrote Wagner of the project.

The imposing six-storey structure is clad in marble, as is customary for banks. However the rivets holding the marble in place are not hidden but ostentatiously exposed and polished as a decorative element that at the same time clearly indicates the function it performs. While this kind of detailing became a common place in later 20th-century architecture, it was a considerable novelty in its own time. The building's reception area was equally original and widely reproduced in architectural handbooks. It features a huge, double-skinned, vaulted glass ceiling (originally intended to be suspended on cables), while its floor is constructed out of glass bricks. A significant feat of engineering for its time, the result was a fresh and light atmosphere that has been emulated many times subsequently in public and corporate buildings.

Wagner sketched many detailed proposals for the transformation of Vienna, but his extensive urban planning ideas stayed largely on the drawing board. One element that did see fruition, however, was the Stadtbahn, or city railway network, for which he and his pupils designed highly decorative stations full of the organic forms that typified Jugendstil (the German version of Art Nouveau). His Majolica House, an apartment block in Vienna (1898) pushed the decorative approach to an extreme, covering the façade in a colourful tiled decoration, from which the house has derived its nickname.

Paradoxically, it was the lack of ornamentation of another project, the Steinhof church build in Vienna in 1906, that more or less finished off Wagner's career after it incurred the wrath of Archduke Franz Ferdinand.

Interior of the Austrian Post Office Savings Bank (1904–12), Wagner's undisputed masterpiece.

Wagner has a dual legacy: for Modernists of succeeding generations, his functional use of material was highly influential, while today he is popular as a proponent of the decorative *fin de siècle* Jugendstil.

Josef Maria Olbrich

The Austrian architect Joseph Maria Olbrich is known principally as a co-founder of the Vienna Secession artistic group, and for designing their exhibition building, the Secession Hall. His work marks the high point of the decorative tendencies of *fin de siècle* Vienna.

Born: 1867, Opava, Czech Republic (then Troppau, Austria)
Importance: Influential member of the Vienna Seccession and designer of its famous exhibition building
Died: 1908, Düsseldorf, Germany

Olbrich studied architecture in Vienna before joining the studio of prominent architect Otto Wagner, where he soon shone. There he is believed to have worked on designs for some highly ornate stations of Vienna's new railway, which are seen as typical examples of Jugendstil, the German version of Art Nouveau.

Through Wagner, Olbrich met a circle of artists and architects with whom he formed the Vienna Secession. The group, which included figures such as the painter Gustav Klimt and architect Josef Hoffman, sought to break away from stultifying academicism to create a freer aesthetic environment.

Olbrich was entrusted with the design of a new dedicated exhibition building for the group, which was financed in part with a donation from the Wittgenstein family. The result was a stunningly original building that is the quintessential expression of the voluptuous style of *fin de siècle* Vienna. Its layout consists of various, cleverly arranged interlocking cubes, but it is the Secession building's decoration that makes it most noteworthy. The ornate, framed entrance is decorated with a frieze showing a glade of trees topped by golden leaves. Above it, like a crown on the roof, there is an ethereal dome made up of yet more gilded bronze leaves. Underneath, written large, is the proclamation *Der Zeit Ihre Kunst, Der Kunst ihre Freiheit* ('To every age its own art, to art its freedom'). The interior decoration is as extensive as the exterior, and includes the *Beethoven Frieze*, one of the most important works of the painter Gustav Klimt.

Close to the beliefs of the anglophone Arts and Crafts Movement and utopian socialism, Olbrich's work was also informed by the notion of a *Gesamptkunstwerk*, or total work of art, an idea promulgated by the composer Richard Wagner, of whom Olbrich was a devoted aficionado.

Olbrich wrote in ecstatic terms of the commission and his desire to create a 'sacred' and 'chaste' building that would be like a Greek temple. His work was criticised for its over-Romanticism, but Olbrich defended the idea of subjective, expressive architecture designed to express the emotions of its creator and evoke positive feelings in those who saw or used it, to bring beauty to everyday life rather than just fulfil a utilitarian function.

This belief in the 'purifying and liberating' aspect of art led to Olbrich designing furniture and household utensils. Olbrich's designs for cutlery and his drawings were as influential as the Secession building and were widely exhibited, even as far afield as the United States, where they caught the eye of Frank Lloyd Wright, who then visited the Matildenhöhe when he visited Europe. Olbrich also designed buildings for a variety of artist colonies or communes, including the Matildenhöhe in Darmstadt, Germany, which he was invited to work on by Ernest Louis, the Grand Duke of Hesse.

Secession Hall (1898), an emblem for the Secession Movement and a Viennese landmark.

Josef Hoffmann

Josef Hoffmann was an important Austrian architect and designer of the early 20th century, whose finely detailed designs were widely influential. Hoffmann's work pioneered a new approach to craft and its accommodation with architecture and he was a co-founder of the Wiener Werkstätter and Deutscher Werkbund design workshops.

Born: 1870, Brtnice, Austria (now in the Czech Republic)
Influence: Pioneer of the role of craft in Modern architecture
Died: 1956, Vienna, Austria

Like Josef Maria Olbrich, to whom he was very close, Hoffmann worked in the studio of Otto Wagner and was also one of the founding members of the Vienna Secession. In contrast to the other young progressive Austrian architects, Hoffmann's career was spent designing luxurious domestic villas and furniture rather than grand public buildings. He is perhaps more appreciated for his interior design and sense of interior space than for the more external aspects of architecture.

More than his Viennese contemporaries, Hoffmann assimilated influences from architects working in other countries, in particular the Scot Charles Rennie Mackintosh and the Belgian Henri van de Velde. They, like many other leading proponents of Art Nouveau, were as adept and interested in the applied arts as monumental architecture, seeing a continuum between the two. And like proponents of the Arts and Crafts movement, Hoffmann believed in the human benefits of craft and introducing beauty to everyday life.

With the backing of a wealthy industrialist, he co-founded the Wiener Werkstätte, or Vienna Workshops, which allowed him to put these ideas into action. Importantly, the exquisitely detailed products emanating from the Wiener Werkstätte, from ceramics to jewellery to pewter tableware, not only carried the name of their designer, but also that of the craftsmen who worked on them. 'Better to work 10 days on one product than to manufacture 10 products in one day', was the motto of the Wiener Werkstätte, the antithesis of modern industrial design. Hoffmann later was a co-founder of the Deutsche Werkbund, a similar organisation in Germany that was, however, more orientated to industrial production.

Hoffmann's most famous building was begun in 1905 for a very wealthy Belgian patron. The Palais Stocklet in Brussels developed a new new language of luxury that would be copied many times. Its panel-like exterior surfacing is clearly influenced by Hoffmann's teacher Otto Wagner, and was admired by Le Corbusier. But the Palais Stocklet owes its fame to the fanatically detailed and ultra-luxurious interior, which recalls the sumptuousness of the palaces of ancient Rome, Byzantium and Egypt.

Hoffmann bequeathed a complex legacy. While his geometric style was an important influence on the international and commercial style of Art Deco in the 1930s, the Wiener Werkstätte also set an important precedent for the avant garde Bauhaus in Germany. His work also carved out a niche for architecture and design that could be both luxurious and modern.

Palais Stocklet, Brussels, set new standards in detail refinement.

Antoni Gaudí

Antoní Gaudí was a startlingly original Catalan architect whose idiosyncratic buildings have come to define the city of Barcelona. Gaudí took the organic forms of Art Nouveau and merged them with elements drawn from Spain's Gothic and Baroque past to create highly unusual buildings that have become extremely popular.

Born: 1852, Reus, Catalonia, Spain
Importance: Hugely original and popular designer who created Barcelona's most famous buildings
Died: 1926, Barcelona, Spain

Born in a small village in Catalonia, Gaudí left to study architecture in Barcelona, where he spent the rest of his life designing buildings that would transform the image of the city forever. A committed vegetarian and devout Catholic, Gaudí's life was as eccentric as the buildings that he designed.

His first works were in the Gothic Revival style but this developed as he was exposed to the Art Nouveau style, which was sweeping across Europe, and began to develop his own inimitable style. Art Nouveau was important for, among other reasons, introducing organic forms drawn from the natural world to the classically straight lines of architecture and design. A lover of the countryside, Gaudí took this element to an unprecedented extreme, creating buildings with sinewy, curvy forms that were more suggestive of the natural world than edifices constructed by humans. The abandonment of the geometric conception of architecture is also indebted to the playfulness of Baroque and Rococo architecture.

For instance, in the Parc Güell (1914), a balcony snakes though the air, decorated with a mosaic of smashed ceramic, incongruously supported by Doric columns. The earlier apartment blocks, Casa Batlló (1905) and Casa Milà (1906), which is

'The straight line belongs to man, the curved line to God.'

affectionately known as La Pedrera, are even more original. The balconies of the former seem to be made from giant animal skeletons, while the curvilinear façade of the latter seems less to be designed than eroded from rock.

Work began on his masterpiece, the church of Sagrada Familia (Holy Family) in 1882. It is an extraordinary assemblage of unusual forms and complex symbolism, Its four main towers (the blueprint calls for 18 in total) rise like spindly elongated ant hills, while the rest of the building is encrusted with bizarre detail. The final decades of Gaudí's career were devoted entirely to the Sagrada Familia and he even spent his last years living in the crypt, before being run over by a tram. The final plans of the building were destroyed during the Spanish Civil War and it remains unfinished, though completion is planned for 2026, the centenary of Gaudí's death.

Gaudí's buildings have always been immensely popular with the general public, but have often been neglected by architects. Only recently have biomorphic forms such as those he investigated become the subject of serious exploration by major designers and architects.

Completion of Sagrada Familia, Gaudí's masterpiece, is planned for 2026.

Adolf Loos

Acknowledged as one of Modernism's most significant pioneers, the Austrian architect Adolf Loos is as famous for his opposition to unnecessary ornamentation as his actual designs. Loos went so far as to compare decoration to crime in his famous 1908 polemic *Ornament and Crime*. 'The evolution of culture is synonymous with the removal of ornament from utilitarian objects', he wrote, arguing that decoration was 'erotic' and even 'degenerate'.

Born: 1870 in Brno, Czech Republic (then part of the Austro-Hungarian Empire)
Importance: Pioneering advocate of unadorned, clean architectural forms
Died: 1933, Vienna, Austria

Loos was born in Brno, then part of the Austro-Hungarian Empire, to humble circumstances. He travelled widely, including to the United States, which impressed him with its modernity. Loos held a variety

The Goldman and Salatsch buiding, also known as Loos Haus (1909–11).

of jobs, including dishwasher and journalist, before settling as an architect in Vienna, the sumptuous Imperial capital, where he spent most of his working life.

Not only was the city full of baroque and imperial structures, but the Secession – the Viennese expression of the Art Nouveau (or Jugendstil) movement – meant voluptuous and florid detail was being applied to everything, from the paintings of Gustav Klimt to the music of Gustav Mahler and buildings of Josef Hoffmann.

Loos was highly critical, arguing that it was important that ornamentation be used appropriately and that utilitarian objects, such as buildings, should be functional and not pretend to be art. The Viennese philosopher Karl Krauss, part of the same cultural circle as Loos, famously quipped that he and Loos had 'done nothing more than show that there is a distinction between an urn and a chamber pot. The others... are divided into those who use the urn as a chamber pot and those who use the chamber pot as an urn.'

Loos's best-known design is the Goldman and Salatsch building in Vienna, usually known as the Loos Haus. Built between 1909 and 1911 on the site of a former baroque building, it occupies a very prominent position in the heart of Vienna, opposite the Imperial residence. Putting his beliefs into action, Loos came up with a radically simple and logical design.

But even as it was being constructed, the clean, unadorned façade of the Loos Haus began to cause outrage for a Viennese public accustomed to highly decorated architecture. Newspapers compared it to a large shed, commentators lined up to complain about the disfigurement of public space and city officials intervened to stop construction. In the end, the façade was left pretty much as Loos intended. While Loos became increasing sidelined, the Goldman and Salatsch building and the debate around it is now widely seen as an epoch-making moment of Modern architecture.

Louis Henri Sullivan

The most important member of the Chicago School of architects, Louis Henri Sullivan spanned the decorative traditions of the 19th century and had a pioneering involvement in the dramatic new genre of the skyscraper, designing some of its most influential early examples.

Born: 1856, Boston, Massachusetts, United States
Importance: Pioneer of steel-framed architecture and the early skyscraper
Died: 1924, Chicago, Illinois, United States

Sullivan had an eclectic architectural education, which included a stint at the Massachusetts Institute of Technology, spells with various different local Chicago architects, and training at the Ecole des Beaux Arts in Paris, during which he was schooled in the dominant ornamental style of 19th-century Europe.

Following the Great Chicago Fire of 1871, the city was extensively redeveloped, with an innovative new structural approach that was to have wide-reaching repercussions for architecture. Rather than relying on brick walls, the architects and structural engineers began to create buildings with load-bearing steel frames, whose strength allowed buildings to safely and easily reach heights impossible before. While Sullivan was not the first to make use of the new technology, he was the first architect to give it its own distinctive language. Working in partnership with German-born Dankmar Adler, Sullivan designed a series of important commercial high-rise buildings utilising metal frames.

The Wainwright Building in St Louis (1890–91) is often seen as the genre's first masterpiece. Eleven stories high, it typically combines structural ingenuity with subtle exterior ornamentation. Vertical elements are accented, and the ground floor and top of the building are treated with contrasting decoration, creating a much-copied template for office buildings in the United States and around the world. The Guaranty Building (now called the Prudential Building) in Buffalo, New York (1894–95) has a similar aesthetic solution to the new high-rise building, but uses the motif of the arch to decorate and articulate its façade.

In 1899, Sullivan, now in practice on his own after falling out with Adler, designed a large corner building for Schleslinger and Mayer, now known as the Sullivan Center. Considered as Sullivan's finest work, the building combines delicate ironwork and a terra cotta decorative exterior tiling with a rational and practical floor plan.

Sullivan was interested in various esoteric philosophies, including Transcendentalism, which was current at the turn of the century. These informed the writings to which he dedicated much of his time as his architectural career declined after the Schleslinger and Mayer building, due in part to a swing in fashion to more conservative architecture. He is now known almost as much for these publications as for what he built. His 1906 essay *The Tall Office Building Artistically Considered* concluded with the oft-quoted line 'form ever follows function', which was to reverberate through the 20th century as the mantra of Modernism. Sullivan also wrote a widely read autobiography entitled *The Autobiography of an Idea*.

While his dictum on form following function, together with his seminal role in the early development of the skyscraper, have assured Sullivan a place in the architectural canon, his presence is also in no small part due to the advocacy of his protégé, Frank Lloyd Wright.

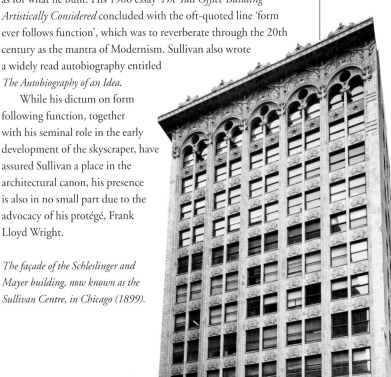

The façade of the Schleslinger and Mayer building, now known as the Sullivan Centre, in Chicago (1899).

SKYSCRAPERS

The skyscraper is the quintessential expression not only of Modernist architecture but perhaps also of the 20th century itself. Like the magnificent Gothic cathedrals of France, this was spectacular architecture designed vertically to deliberately inspire awe and wonder.

The origins of the skyscraper lie in the ingenuity of the architects and structural engineers involved in the rebuilding of Chicago in the 1870s and 1880s. Rather than rely on conventional brick walls, they began to utilise load-bearing steel skeletons, whose immense strength allowed buildings to reach previously undreamt of heights. Concurrent technological developments, most notably the elevator, made these multi-storey buildings practical to use, and they quickly became expressions of corporate might and ambition. 'It must be tall. The force and power of altitude must be in it, the glory and power of altitude must be in it', wrote Louis H. Sullivan, one of the pioneering Chicago architects, in 1896.

The most important early example of a building using the novel construction method is the 10-storey Home Insurance Building in Chicago (1884), designed by William LeBaron Jenney. It was greeted by public wonderment and led to the term skyscraper gaining common currency. Manhattan's first important example of a skyscraper was the 22-storey Flatiron Building erected in 1902 and designed by Chicago architect Daniel Burnham.

In a rivalry that would hark back to the *campanilismo* of the Medieval Italian city states, whose civic pride depended on having the taller towers, Chicago and New York competed to build ever taller buildings. New York's two best-loved skyscrapers were conceived in the boom years of the 1920s. The elegant, Art Deco-influenced, 320m (1,050ft) Chrysler building, designed by William van Alen in 1928, was quickly followed by the Empire State Building, begun in 1930 and designed by Shreve, Lamb & Harmon Associates. At 380m (1,247ft) high and with a record 102 storeys, it held the crown as the world's tallest structure until the erection of the Sears Tower in Chicago in 1974.

These skyscrapers were emulated around the world, often in the financial districts of major cities. A practical response to expensive ground rents, they were also prestigious corporate statements. Important recent examples include the César Pelli-designed Petronas Twin Towers in Kuala Lumpur, Malaysia (erected in 1992–98) and 30 St Mary's Axe in London, England (2004), designed by Foster and Partners, which is popularly known as the Gherkin due to its unorthodox conical shape.

> '*It must be every inch a proud and soaring thing, rising in sheer exaltation that from bottom to top it is a unit without a single dissenting line.*'
>
> Louis Henri Sullivan

At over 800m (2,625ft), the Burj Dubai in the new financial district of Dubai is, as of 2009, the tallest building in the world. Its designers, Skidmore, Owings and Merrill, a practice famous for its skyscrapers, took inspiration from a utopian sketch by Frank Lloyd Wright of a skyscraper that would stretch one mile into the sky.

While skyscrapers defined the optimism of the 20th century, the catastrophic demise of the Twin Towers, the iconic towers of Manhattan's World Trade Centre, in the tragic events of 11 September 2001, marked the inauguration of a new, troubled era.

Frank Lloyd Wright

Commonly accepted as America's greatest architect, Frank Lloyd Wright was also one of its most prolific. He designed some 500 buildings, including some of modern America's most iconic structures, tempering audacious gestures and eclectic influences with a deep respect for nature.

Born: 1867, Richland Center, Wisconsin, United States
Importance: Creator of a distinctively American form of Modernism
Died: 1959, Phoenix, Arizona, United States

An unconventional figure even as a youth, Wright appears not to have gained any formal educational or architectural qualifications. He left his native Wisconsin for Chicago and its building boom, where he worked briefly for the firm of Adler & Sullivan in Chicago, developing a life-long respect for Louis Sullivan.

He set up his own practice in 1893 after being sacked for moonlighting, Wright was soon busy designing residential homes in the 'prairie style', the name being derived from the landscape near Chicago on which they were built. Like Greene and Greene and Charles Rennie Mackintosh, Wright was entranced by Japanese architecture, and incorporated elements from it to create novel architectural forms. Westcott House in Springfield, Ohio (1908), for instance, is clearly influenced by a traditional Japanese Buddhist temple.

Wright's first masterpiece, and best example of his early 'prairie' style, is the Frederick C. Robie House (1908–10) in Chicago. It features dramatically cantilevered roof lines that extend over large parts of the property. Its accentuation of the horizontal and creation of overlapping spaces give the building a relaxed and open air.

While the Robie House was being built, Wright travelled to Europe, where, in Berlin, he arranged for his buildings to be

'Study nature, love nature, stay close to nature. It will never fail you.'

published by Wasmuth, and they were greeted by international acclaim. He soon returned to the United States and, after a tumultuous period, re-established his architectural practice.

Fallingwater (1934–37) is his finest domestic building and justly famous. Designed for a wealthy publishing magnate, it makes the fullest possible use of its remote location over a river in rural Pennsylvania. Cantilevered concrete balconies seem to hang from a rough stone-clad centre in such a way as to seem part

Fallingwater (1934–37) is one of the best-known buildings of the 20th century.

of the waterfall itself. In seeming to become part of the landscape, Fallingwater exemplified the 'organicist' principles that Wright espoused.

His late masterpiece is the Solomon G. Guggenheim Museum in New York, which was begun in 1943 and opened in 1959, the year of his death. Instantly recognisable, the building is like a giant upside-down snail shell. Visitors to the art museum travel to the top of the building by elevator and then descend a diminishing spiral ramp, alongside which the art works are displayed. The organic curves of the building's exterior contrast with the otherwise rectilinear nature of New York.

The architecture of Wright was immensely influential internationally. His careful 'organic' integration of a building to its surroundings and respect for nature provided an important alternative example to the strictures of Le Corbusier and his followers.

Gerrit Rietveld

Gerrit Rietveld was a highly original architect and furniture designer, who rigorously introduced the aesthetic philosophy of the influential De Stijl movement to design. The extreme abstraction of the Schöder House in particular was one of the seminal moments in the development of Modernist architecture.

Born: 1888, Utrecht, Netherlands
Importance: First exponent of the extreme geometric simplicity that would become central to Modernism
Died: 1964, Utrecht, Netherlands

Rietveld's initial training was in cabinet making and jewellery design, but after setting up his own furniture company, he began to study architecture. In 1917, he designed his now-famous Red Blue geometric chair and began to associate with the avant garde De Stijl group.

De Stijl was an important movement of early Modernism, taking its name from the journal edited by Theo van Doesburg, the group's leader. Its utopian principles of aesthetic harmony and abstraction led its practitioners to restrict themselves to straight lines and a palette of colours that included only the primary colours, black and white. Its most famous practitioner was the painter Piet Mondrian, but this radical aesthetic was applied to furniture design and architecture by Rietveld with far-reaching consequences.

The Schröder House is a villa in a suburb of Utrecht designed by Rietveld in 1924 in close association with its owner Truus Schröder-Schräder, a radically minded young widow. The house is considered the only strict application of the principles of De Stijl to an architectural brief, and is often compared to a three-dimensional Mondrian painting. It is conceived sculpturally as a very tight aesthetically defined space, in which there are only single planes and right angles. Famously, its window would be kept open only at a right angle, so as not to disturb the overall effect of the geometric design.

This was stark abstraction and rigorous geometry taken to a new level, and was to become a distinguishing feature of Modernist architecture.

Another feature that was emulated by later Modernist architects is to be found on the villa's top floor, described by Rietveld as 'the attic'. Here, movable screens, rather than fixed walls, create a space that is open and light and can be reconfigured at will by its inhabitants.

In his later years, Rietveld moved away from the extremes of De Stijl, designing buildings that lacked the startling originality of the Schröder House. The most important building of these years is the Van Gogh Museum in Amsterdam, erected posthumously in 1973.

Rietveld's early work, and in particular the highly acclaimed Schröder House, was an important influence for two of the greatest architects of the century, Le Corbusier and Mies van der Rohe. He paved the way to a completely new architectural vocabulary that would define the century.

Schröder House, the only strict architectural application of De Stijl principles.

Le Corbusier

After Palladio, Le Corbusier is probably the single most celebrated and most influential of all architects. His varied projects, embodying different strands of Modernism, tower over the architecture of the 20th century.

Born: 1887, La-Chaux-de-Fonds, Switzerland
Importance: Creator of a new paradigm of Modernist architecture
Died: 1965, Roquebrune-Cap-Martin, France

After early years spent travelling and assimilating different influences, from which he would distil the most potent and influential line of Modernist architecture, Le Corbusier, born Charles-Édouard Jeanneret in Switzerland, spent the majority of his working life in France.

In 1923, he published *Vers une architecture* (*Towards a New Architecture*), a manifesto of Modernist architecture that became obligatory reading for progressive architects around the world. In it, he set out his utopian ideals, inspired by Communism: he believed architecture and technology could be efficiently combined to create a more equitable future. Architecture, he wrote, should be functional rather than stylistic, designed as a 'machine for living'. Le Corbusier took the new construction methods of concrete and steel and, more than any other architect, used them to create a new architectural language that would be emulated repeatedly through the century.

The most important example of his early, Purist work is the Villa Savoye (1928–31). Situated on the outskirts of Paris, it synthesises a new Classicism (its form is indebted to the Greek temple) with a novel and very contemporary paradigm of the modern house. Its clean lines and elegant beauty, together with its innovative interior layout (including a ramp rather than staircase) has made it one of the most famous of 20th century buildings. Its white abstract forms make it the best example of what became known as the International Style.

Villa Savoye, the most famous example of the International Style.

In the most important project of his middle career, the Unité d'Habitation in Marseilles (1946–52), Le Corbusier was able to fuse his ideas about rationalisation and city planning. The 12-story apartment building provides housing for 1,600, with different-size apartments slotted in, and is probably the most imitated of all post-war social housing projects. Its rough-poured concrete also gave rise to a trend in architecture known as Brutalism.

The Chapel Notre-Dame-du-Haut (usually known by the name of its location, Ronchamps) marks a radical change of direction but is as admired as his earlier designs. Instead of relying on machine aesthetics, its organic, sculptural forms are inspired by Surrealist art.

Le Corbusier's impact on 20th-century architecture and planning can scarcely be overstated – every architect knows his major projects in detail. And while he was seen as the high priest of a cold machine-like aesthetic later criticised as inhuman, others of his projects, notably the Ronchamps, point towards Post-Modernism and beyond with their free, expressive, sculptural forms.

INTERNATIONAL STYLE
The International Style describes the mature form of architectural Modernism prevalent in the middle of the 20th century. It is characterised by pared down rectilinear forms, often painted white, the use of concrete, glass and steel, and is epitomized by Le Corbusier's Villa Savoye

MODERNISM

Modernism was the most important cultural movement of the 20th century and the dominant influence on its architecture. Lasting from the turn of the century until the 1970s, Modernism describes a common mind set shared by progressive, or avant garde (to use a typical Modernist term), practitioners, who sought to positively engage with the newly industrialised and mechanised world and the needs of its recent large urban populations.

In the arts, the most important Modernists include Franz Kafka and James Joyce in literature, Arnold Schoenberg and Igor Stravinsky in music, and Pablo Picasso and Wassily Kandinsky in painting. In architecture, it is triumvirate of Le Corbusier, Walter Gropius and Ludwig Mies van der Rohe who are considered the seminal Modernists, and they spearheaded a new kind of architecture that was soon disseminated internationally.

While artists looked to figures such as Sigmund Freud to understand the fragmented subjectivities of man in the new urban environment, architects instead tended to focus on the political philosophy of Karl Marx, which lent Modernist architecture a strong social conscience. Many of the leading Modernist architects, if not Communists themselves, were inspired by its beliefs and the 1917 Russian Revolution. For most Modernists, architecture was not just about designing buildings, but about creating new social realities, new forms in which modern life could take place. Modernist architects fervently believed that technology was an agent for good and that their role was a practical and functional one, summed up by the oft repeated mantra 'form follows function'.

The Ville Contemporaine (Contemporary City) that Le Corbusier exhibited as sketches in 1922 encapsulates many features of the Modernist architectural project. It presents a futuristic, rectilinear, 'ideal' city for three million inhabitants, who would live in glass skyscrapers and travel along elevated roads. While it was never built, its vision of high-density living in uniform blocks and a total mechanisation of space proved extremely influential and informed smaller schemes by Modernist architects around the world.

Modernism was not initially a style but a philosophy. However, its inherent formal features – rational and transparent construction using 'modern' materials such as concrete, steel and glass, a lack of ornament, open-plan layouts, flat roofs and simple, clearly expressed geometric forms – were soon assimilated into what would be known by the 1930s as the International Style (taking its name from a seminal 1932 exhibition in New York).

With the arrival in the United States of many of the leading European Modernist architects in the 1930s and 1940s, later Modernist

> *'The house is a machine for living.'*
> Le Corbusier

architecture lost much of its initial utopian zeal and began to focus more on these formal elements in response to commissions from corporations wishing to present a modern face to the world. In other parts of the world, Modernism continued to heavily influence social housing projects. Although well intentioned, these were sometimes poorly executed and they have now largely fallen into disrepute.

By early 1970s, Modernism had largely run its course, both aesthetically and philosophically. In the 1990s, Neo-Modernist architecture came to the fore, practised by contemporary architects such as Norman Foster, using many of the formal elements of Modernist architecture, such as glass exterior walls, but now to purely formal and commercial ends.

Founder of the Bauhaus
Walter Gropius

German architect Walter Gropius is one of the most important and influential of Modern architects, pioneering a new structural approach that allowed the greater use of glass and flat roofs. His leadership of the Bauhaus saw a whole generation of designers and architects schooled in Modernism.

Born: 1883, Berlin, Germany
Importance: Founder of the influential Bauhaus and pioneer of Modernist architecture
Died: 1969, Cambridge, Massachusetts, United States

Gropius came into contact with other future luminaries of Modernist architect, Le Corbusier and Mies van der Rohe, while studying with the important German architect Peter Behrens, whose AEG factory of 1907 revolutionised industrial architecture and gave birth to the modern notion of corporate identity.

Gropius's first important commission was also a factory – the Fagus Werke (1911) in Hanover. The structure (designed together with Adolf Meyer) took Behrens' ideas one stage

The Dessau Bauhaus: Gropius founded the school and designed its building.

further. Here, glazing entirely dominates the façade, which seems a curtain of glass, and continues around the corners without any obvious structural support. This was a dramatic and radical innovation that was conspicuously technological, and the 'curtain wall' became an almost paradigmatic feature of future Modernist buildings.

Gropius succeeded Belgian architect Henri van der Velde as leader of the Grand Ducal School of Arts and Crafts in Weimar. Under his enlightened stewardship, the school was transformed into the Bauhaus, and some of the 20th century's greatest talents, including Wassily Kandinsky, Paul Klee, Josef Albers, Herbert Bayer and Ludwig Mies van der Rohe, were assembled to inculcate students with the latest Modernism thinking.

In 1925, Gropius moved the school to Dessau and designed its new home – an iconic building whose external features signalled the Modernist design education taking place inside. Another landmark of modern architecture, the building likewise features an impressive glass exterior wall. Its two large flat-roofed blocks are connected by a bridge-like smaller building supported on slender columns.

After Hitler seized power, Gropius emigrated to the United States, where he built himself a house in Lincoln, Massachusetts. This structure, and his teaching at Harvard, introduced the latest advances in European Modernist architecture to the United States.

The most important project of Gropius's later years, the Pan-Am Building (since renamed the MetLife Building), constructed in 1963 and designed by Gropius in conjunction with Emery Roth & Sons and Pietro Belluschi, has not always been critically regarded as a success. It is a 58-storey skyscraper that hovers above Central Station, dominating the heart of Manhattan. Its blocky appearance, often criticised as plain and heavy, is however typical of many post-war commercial buildings.

While his later career may not have yielded the impressive results of his youth, his earlier achievements make Gropius absolutely central to 20th-century design and the Modernist project. As a pedagogue and founder of the seminal Bauhaus, his influence reached right through Modernist architecture and design.

Ludwig Mies van der Rohe

Along with Le Corbusier and Walter Gropius, Ludwig Mies van der Rohe is one of the pillars of Modern architecture. While the other two were social visionaries as much as architects,

Born: 1886, Aachen, Germany
Importance: Exemplary and much emulated practitioner of formalist trend in Modernism
Died: 1969, Chicago, Illinois, United States

Mies van der Rohe exemplified another aspect of Modernist architecture – a rigorous paring down of forms and fastidious attention to detail.

Like his two famous contemporaries, Mies van der Rohe studied with Peter Behrens before establishing his own practice, designing a series of airy Modernist villas that relied primarily on sumptuous materials for their decoration. Their success led to the invitation to design the German Pavilion for the International Exposition held in Barcelona in 1929. The masterpiece he produced is one of the high points of Modernist design.

Since reconstructed and now known as the Barcelona Pavilion, it is a deceptively simple structure, in which slabs of marble and precious stone alternate with floor-to-ceiling glass walls to define an ethereal yet luxurious environment. The ambiguous space dissolves the distinction between inside and out. Other than a large water feature, the space is minimally furnished, with just a single statue and Mies van der Rohe's now iconic Barcelona chair.

Like many other progressive cultural figures, Mies van der Rohe left Nazi Germany for the United States in 1937, living in Chicago for the rest of his life. On the strength of his already considerable international reputation, he was appointed Head of Architecture of what is now the Illinois Institute of Technology. Mies van der Rohe was also commissioned to master-plan its campus and design some of its buildings, including the Crown Hall (1950), an ethereal glass block that seems to effortlessly exist with support from four large steel

The Barcelona Pavilion, famous for its simple form and sumptuous materials.

girders. It exemplifies the structural simplicity and clear articulation for which he became so renowned.

Equally severe and minimal is the Farnsworth House, built in 1945–51 for a wealthy client in Plano, Illinois, which took the rarified design elements of the Barcelona Pavilion and applied them to a holiday home. The house is almost entirely transparent, on account of its glass walls, and it seems almost to float above the meadow where it is located. While it pushed the Modernist idiom to a new extreme, the building proved to be as famous for high-profile litigation between client and architect as for its design.

His 1958 New York Seagram Building is his late masterpiece and widely seen as one of the greatest skyscrapers. It was expensively clad in bronze and tinted glass and has the luxury of its own plaza replete with fountains. Deceptively simple, the 38-storey structure manages to be refined and subtle and yet maintain its own identity in the noise of Manhattan's architecture. Its meticulous choice of materials and obsessively controlled detailing – encapsulated by Mies van der Rohe's famous assertion that 'less is more' – was characteristic of his work, and set an important precedent for future Minimalists.

JJP Oud

Considered one of the founding fathers of Modernist architecture, Jacobus Johannes Pieter Oud is best known for the influential buildings he designed in the early part of his long and varied career, particularly his designs for three major social housing projects in the 1920s.

Born: 1890, Purmerend, Netherlands
Importance: Pioneer of Modernist social housing
Died: 1963, Wassenaar, Netherlands

Oud initially wanted to become a painter but studied architecture at the insistence of his father, and spent time in London and Munich, where he worked with the innovative architect Theodor Fischer. He also took an interest in American architects Louis Sullivan and Frank Lloyd Wright and was in close contact with Belgian architect Henry van de Velde, distilling these various influences and approaches into his own functional style.

Like Gerrit Rietveld, he was initially part of the Dutch avant garde movement, De Stijl, formed in 1917, and although he didn't apply its strictures with anything like the same severity, the De Stijl aesthetic is clearly discernible in the oversized graphic treatment of the façade of the Café De Unie (1925) in Rotterdam.

In 1918, at the young age of 28, Oud was appointed Municipal Housing Architect for the city of Rotterdam. In this role, he was able to bring the functional design philosophy and clean lines of Modernist architecture to bear on large schemes to provide social housing for the working classes. The two most important examples are the Hook of Holland Estate (1927) and Kiefhoek Housing Estate (1930). These estates revolutionised social housing with their simple, whitewashed, streamlined shapes and rationalised layout. The Hook of Holland Estate featured two-storey terraced houses with integral balconies, demonstrating the way in which Modernist principles could be applied to create effective and desirable social housing.

His work led to international recognition, and in 1927, he was invited by Ludwig Mies van der Rohe to contribute designs for the Weissenhof Estate, an ambitious assemblage of social housing in Stuttgart, Germany. Built as part of an exhibition staged by the Deutscher Werkbund, the 21 houses by different architects were intended as a showcase of exemplary designs that could improve the lot of the common man. Oud's design was an exceptionally cleanly designed terrace of five houses.

In 1933, he left his municipal post to set up his own practice, but didn't produce any buildings of note, despite being internationally feted, including by American architect Philip Johnson, who commissioned him to design a house for his mother that was never built. In 1938, he designed Shell's headquarters in The Hague, but its ornamental style cause consternation among progressive architects.

While Oud's star shone brightly at the start of his career, his work did not develop with the richness of that of his contemporaries Le Corbusier, Mies van der Rohe or Walter Gropius. Nevertheless, his social housing schemes set a new standard, and their influence is discernible in projects around the world well into the 1970s.

Social housing at its Modernist best: Oud's design for the Weissenhof Estate.

THE ARCHITECTURE OF FASCIST ITALY AND NAZI GERMANY

Accounts of the architecture of the 20th century are overwhelmingly dominated by the trajectory of Modernism and its various offshoots. However, in the totalitarian regimes of Mussolini in Italy and Adolf Hitler in Germany (as well as in Stalinist Russia), a very different kind of monumental architecture developed. While certain technological elements were appropriated from Modernism, its overwhelming characteristic was a new kind of ceremonial Classicising.

It is well known that Hitler was a frustrated artist and fanatically interested in architecture; he discussed the subject at length in his autobiography *Mein Kampf.* On his assumption of power in 1933, Hitler sought to reinvent Germany in the image of Ancient Greece, inspired by the example of 19th-century Hellenism and the Neo-Classical architect Karl Friedrich Schinkel in particular. Modernist architecture was seen as a Jewish or Bolshevist conspiracy.

Hitler's first architectural adviser, Paul Ludwig Troost, was responsible for the Haus der Kunst (1934–36), an art gallery in Munich that is a grandiose and austere reinterpretation of a Doric Temple. The rigid conformity and repetition of its columns along with the building's ability to act as a foil for the propaganda of the National Socialists established a formal language that would typify the most notorious of the grand building designs of the Third Reich.

This was most fully exploited by Albert Speer, who succeeded Troost following the latter's death in 1934. Speer famously saw architecture as a kind of theatrical backdrop, an idea that was most fully expressed in his gigantic design for the Zeppelinfeld, in which the Nuremberg rallies were staged with almost religious fervour. Speer also drew up grand plans to remodel Berlin and Hitler's home city of Linz, and in 1938, designed the New Reich Chancellery that became Hitler's new headquarters. The building's enormous size and extensive use of marble was a deliberate expression of power and domination.

In the grandiose plans for a 'thousand year Reich', it was seen as important that quality materials, primarily marble, be used for the monumental architecture, so that the buildings would exist for posterity as beautiful ruins, according to Speer's infamous *Ruinenwerttheorie* (ruin value theory).

In Fascist Italy there was a similar turn to a hard, contemporary Neo-Classicism. The Vittore Emanuele II Monument, a large white temple-like structure hacked into the centre of Rome and completed in 1935, is as pompous and stodgy as anything produced in Nazi Germany. However, a less bombastic and more simplified vein of Classicism also emerged. Its quintessential expression is the Palazzo della Civiltà Italiana, designed by Giovanni Guerrini, Ernesto La Padula and Mario Romano for the 1942 Universal Exhibition as an exemplary demonstration of Fascist architecture. Its rhythmical, travertine-clad

> *'If the creative spirit of the Periclean age be manifested in the Parthenon, then the Bolshevist era is manifested through its cubist grimace.'*
> Adolf Hitler

façade combines classical and modern elements in a way that would prefigure the work of later Post-Modernists.

This refined Classicism, sharing some of the surreal qualities of the paintings of Giorgio de Chirico, is also evident in the work of Giuseppe Terragni, in particular his widely admired 1936 regional headquarters for the Fascists in Como, the Case del Fascio.

Marcel Breuer

A close associate of Walter Gropius, the Hungarian architect Marcel Breuer designed unpretentious and subtly detailed buildings that exemplified the International Style. With Gropius and Ludwig Mies van der Rohe, Breuer was responsible for introducing this new Modern architecture to the United States.

Born: 1902, Pécs, Hungary
Importance: Functionalist Modernist
Died: 1981, New York City, New York, United States

As a graduate of the Bauhaus, Breuer was well schooled in the innovations of nascent Modernism. In keeping with the interdisciplinary ethos of the Bauhaus, Breuer taught carpentry. He pioneered the tubular-steel furniture that is emblematic of Modernism, most famously the 'Wassily' chair, so named because it was admired by Breuer's Bauhaus colleague, the Russian abstract painter Wassily Kandinsky.

This same craft sensibility is apparent in his buildings. While vigorously functional and beautifully detailed, Breuer's architecture distances itself from the more austere elements of Modernism that are rightly or wrongly associated with Le Corbusier. As Breuer pointedly said of his buildings, 'you want to have something simpler, more elemental, more generous, and more human than a machine'.

As Modernism came under pressure from the National Socialists in Germany, Breuer followed his erstwhile teacher Gropius first to London and then to the United States, joining him in teaching and practice at Harvard. In 1946, he set up his own practice in New York.

Breuer's initial commissions in the United States were for a succession of innovative residential buildings. He was quickly able to assimilate indigenous New England architecture to his imported European High Modernism, as is apparent in the timber-framed Chamberlain Cottage designed in 1940.

The commission to design the European headquarters of UNESCO in Paris in 1953 reaffirmed his international standing. Designed in conjunction with Bernard Zehrfuss and Pier Luigi Nervi, the elegant solution to the difficult site was a curving 'Y'-shaped structure. The building was made of reinforced concrete, but its curved shape, a typical feature of Breuer's later architecture, softened its impact.

The St John's Abbey Church, finished in 1961, is the most complex of Breuer's sculptural experiments in concrete architecture. The main building alternates between heavy

Witney Museum of American Art, Manhattan (1966).

columns and a honeycomb wall, while its freestanding belfry, also made of reinforced concrete, has an unusually flattened form.

This freer approach, loosening the rigours of Modernism, is also evident in the Whitney Museum of American Art in Manhattan. Completed in 1966, it features a heavy granite façade with progressively cantilevered overhangs punctured by an irregularly shaped window. While the subject of much controversy as it was built, the building is now probably Breuer's best-known work.

Breuer's legacy lies not in single, innovative, high-profile buildings but rather in the detail of the careful, considered designs of his corpus as a whole. Through his teaching and practice, American architects such as Philip Johnson and IM Pei received a European Modernist schooling and the tools with which to create a specifically American modern architecture.

Berthold Lubetkin

Founder of the influential Tecton group, Russian-born architect Berthold Lubetkin introduced Modernist architecture to Britain. His combination of Constructivist and High Modernist principles were developed into a distinctive form of Modernism that would for decades characterise many major British projects.

Born: 1901, Tbilisi, Georgia (then Russia)
Importance: Introduced and championed Modernist architecture in Britain
Died: 1990, Bristol, UK

Born in Tbilisi, Lubetkin moved to Moscow to study art, witnessing the Russian Revolution of 1917 first hand, and remaining wedded to the passion for social justice that fuelled it for the rest of his life. In Moscow, he was able to imbibe the radical theories of Constructivists such as Naum Gabo and Vladimir Tatlin, which combined social commitment with a futuristic machine aesthetic. He moved to Paris, where he came into contact with Le Corbusier and studied with his teacher Auguste Perret, learning the novel concrete construction methods that underpinned Modernism.

In 1930, unwilling to return to a Russia in the hands of Stalin, he accepted an invitation to come to Britain. While Modern architecture was at its height during the 1920s in Germany and France, Britain was an architectural backwater. Largely untouched by the radical new architecture of mainland Europe, British buildings were mainly of traditional design and construction. Not only were commissions hard to come by, but planning constraints made the permission to construct Modernist buildings very difficult to obtain.

Together with six British architects, Lubetkin established Tecton in London, and, with celebrated Danish structural engineer Ove Arup, he began to design concrete structures that would revolutionise British architecture. The first major commissions were for a succession of zoo buildings, including one, in 1933, for what would become one of his most famous works – the Penguin Pool for London Zoo. This stunning structure included two interlocking curved ramps in a virtuoso display of the new technology and architecture.

Highpoint One, completed in 1935, was the first of two major residential blocks in Highgate, North London. It introduced the full rigours of Corbusian architecture to Britain. A starkly modelled, flat-roofed, concrete high-rise, making much of the wide-ranging views the site enabled, it was praised by Le Corbusier himself on a visit to London.

In 1938, Lubetkin designed a health centre for Finsbury Council, a left-wing North London local authority. Its modern materials became symbolic of the struggle to improve the lives of ordinary Londoners and its success led Finsbury to ask Lubetkinto draw up plans to regenerate the area. These were, however, interrupted by World War II.

Penguin Pool, London Zoo (1933): a simple brief translated into a stunning structure.

Lubetkin's new style of architecture was exemplarily matched to the post-war Labour government with its radical agenda. In 1946, Aneurin Bevan, founder of the NHS and the modern British welfare state, laid the foundation stone of Spa Green Estate, one of a series of important public housing schemes that relied on prefabricated concrete and cost-effective construction methods.

Lubetkin soon grew disgruntled at planning difficulties and retired to his country farm, but his earlier buildings had served to establish a distinctive form of Modernism that would characterise the post-war reconstruction of Britain.

Philip Johnson

An eclectic and controversial populariser of various architectural styles, Philip Johnson is one of the most important 20th-century American architects. He managed to be at the centre of architectural debates thoughout a long and varied career that spanned High Modernism of the 1930s through to Post-Modernism in the 1980s.

Born: 1906, Cleveland, Ohio, United States
Importance: Eclectic Modernist who became a leading Post-Modernist architect
Died: 2005, New Canaan, Connecticut, United States

Johnson is one of architecture's late starters, reaching the age of 43 before he designed his first building. He had previously been an academic, curator and architectural critic, whose catalogue for the 1932 show at the Museum of Modern Art in New York, the International Style, had been seminal in creating a worldwide audience for progressive French and German Modernist architects.

Designed as part of his Master's degree, his first building, was, however, a masterpiece. The Glass House, which he constructed for himself in New Canaan in 1949, took ideas from Ludwig Mies van der Rohe and developed them to a previously unimagined extreme. Famously having views for walls, the transparent structure is basically a glass cube set upon a shallow base.

Despite this homage to Mies van der Rohe and close collaboration with the German master on his seminal Seagram skyscraper in New York, Johnson's inquiring mind and restless imagination led to a dissatisfaction with the strictures of European Modernism, whose left-wing political underpinnings were, in any case, anathema to him. Impractical yet beautiful, the Glass House began a critical engagement with Modernism that would cause continuing controversy. In Johnson's hand, Modernism was seen as an ensemble of formal effects shorn of their underlying theoretical basis, which were then pressed into service to create various novel forms of contemporary American architecture, from Minimalist to Post-Modern.

His most prolific period was from 1967 to 1987, when he went into practice with John Burgee. A series of large-scale buildings, mainly in the United States, developed a brash, eclectic style that was instrumental in the development of what would be termed Post-Modernism.

The AT&T Building (now the Sony Building), completed in 1984, outraged Modernists with its ornamental Chippendale pediment and has become one of Post-Modernism's most infamous buildings.

The slightly earlier Crystal Cathedral (1980), in Southern California, has become a landmark in its own way. An enormous structure capable of housing 2,700 worshippers, it was considered by Johnson to be his masterpiece. Its unusual construction consists of 10,000 panes of reflective glass glued to delicate steel trusses, with two 27.4m (90ft) electronically operated doors that allow the sunlight and breezes in at opportune moments.

By the time of his death at the age of 98 (in his own Glass House), Johnson was still a controversial figure. Assimilator and disseminator of many, often conflicting, architectural styles, Johnson remains a problematic figure for many, who see him as an exemplar of superficial architecture in the service of fashion. Yet his influence on contemporary US architecture is undeniable and attested to by the considerable number of important buildings designed by him.

AT&T Building (now the Sony Building), New York (1984).

Gio Ponti

Gio Ponti played an important role in establishing Italy's design eminence in the 20th century. He worked with equal ability and influence in architecture, industrial design and journalism. During a long and prolific career, he designed buildings in various idioms, most notably developing a characteristically Italian version of Modern architecture in the years of post-war reconstruction.

Born: 1891, Milan, Italy
Importance:
Established the post-war pre-eminence of Italian design
Died: 1979, Milan, Italy

After a period studying architecture at the Milan Polytechnic, interrupted by service in World War I, Ponti worked in a series of practices, coming to prominence on account of his journalism and industrial design as much as for his early architecture. Most significantly, he co-founded the influential design and architecture magazine *Domus*, which he continued to edit for much of his life.

Several major projects after World War II put Ponti's architecture on the international map. The Villa Planchart in Caracas, Venezuela, is one of the most influential private home designs of the 20th century. For its wealthy owners, Ponti created a villa that beautifully integrates the graceful outside with a luxurious interior, which he designed down to the tiniest detail. The building's perforated exterior creates an effect of lightness and delicacy that typify Ponti's architecture.

Also in 1956, construction began on Ponti's most important architectural achievement, the Pirelli Tower. Designed in conjunction with Pier Luigi Nervi and Alberto Rosselli, the 32-storey glass-clad edifice for the Italian tyre and plastics manufacturer presented a new elegant approach to the skyscraper that was quite distinct from its forthright American counterparts. Rather than use a steel frame, it is constructed of reinforced concrete, and instead of a box form, it features angled corners that create ambiguous shapes depending on the angle from which the tower is viewed.

In 2002, the Pirelli Tower (which now houses local government offices) survived a light aeroplane crashing into it. This widely publicised tragedy inaugurated a re-evaluation of the building and a cleaning program that restored the exterior to its original elegance.

The critical plaudits that greeted the Pirelli Tower led to a variety of commissions internationally, from Iraq (the Ministry of Planning, 1958) to the United States (the Denver Art Museum, 1971). The most important Italian architectural projects of Ponti's latter years, however, are predominately ecclesiastic. These include the Milanese churches of San Francesco (1964) and San Carlo (1967), and a cathedral for the Southern Italian city of Taranto (1970) that features a delicate, filigree façade.

Ponti's work in industrial design was perhaps even more influential than his architecture, and items he designed such as the curved, chromed espresso machine for La Pavoni and the Superleggera chair have become iconic of Modern Italy. His product design, together with his journalism, helped to establish Italy, and Milan in particular, as a centre of design excellence, a reputation that it continues to enjoy today.

The Pirelli Tower (1956–60) was the first skyscraper in Italy and is now a Milanese landmark.

Alvar Aalto

One of the major figures of International Modernism, Alvar Aalto is the best known and most influential of a generation that established a specifically Scandinavian brand of Modern architecture. His designs blended local traditional elements and materials, notably wood, with the latest developments in international architecture to novel and enduring effect.

Born: 1898, Kuortane, Finland
Importance: Pioneer of Scandinavian Modernism
Died: 1976, Helsinki, Finland

Aalto was fortunate to begin practising as an architect during the years when Finland was rebuilding itself after regaining independence from Russia in 1917. Though Aalto himself was a flamboyant showman, his designs exemplify Scandinavian understatement and restraint. They also expressed a wish to connect and integrate with the natural world. Rather than the machine aesthetic espoused by the leading German and French architects, Aalto's designs prioritised simplicity, the wellbeing of their users and, above all, a harmonious relationship with the natural world. This last aspect he shared with Frank Lloyd Wright, one of many major architects to praise his work.

While Aalto enjoyed a long and industrious career, he is particularly prized by architects for a handful of early buildings. The Palmio Sanitorium (1929–33), in particular, is seen as one of the very finest of buildings in the International Modern style, tempering formal perfection and impeccable detailing with an uncommon receptivity to the needs of its users. The sensitive yet rational use of space and the large windows of the building, which is set in the middle of a forest, were much copied by later 20th century hospital buildings.

The celebrated Viipuri Library (1933–35) pushed this humanistic element further. Its most famous feature is an undulating wood-panelled suspended ceiling. Designed for acoustic effect, it also created an organic and warm human environment. It was also for this space that Aalto designed his famous and immensely popular three-legged bent-wood stool.

However, perhaps the most representative building of Aalto's early career is the Villa Mairea (1937–39). Wooden poles and walls are integrated with sharp white brick walls and masonry to create a seamless integration with its natural environment, and its informal yet pristine aesthetic has become emblematic of Nordic design.

Some of Aalto's later projects have also proved very influential, such as the Säynätsalo Town Hall (1952), whose use of exposed

The porcelain-tile-clad exterior of Seinajoki Town Hall (1962–66).

brick to express Modernist shapes proved popular with later generations of architects seeking an alternative to concrete.

In 1935, Aalto co-founded the furniture company Artek, which still sells the kind of Scandanavian Modernist products he designed. Many of Aalto's own product designs continue to be phenomenally successful, particularly the wave-shaped glass Savoy vase. But while Aalto may generally be better known for these smaller-scale designs, his architecture has always been held in very high esteem by his peers. Recent years have witnessed a revival of interest in his work by architects, including Shigeru Ban, who are seeking to develop a more ecological approach.

SOCIAL HOUSING

With the development of Socialism out of the injustices of the Industrial Revolution, the provision of social housing for the poor and disadvantaged became a major political concern. Provided either by local government or by enlightened employers, it created a new category of communal building.

Early British and Dutch examples were heavily influenced by the Arts and Crafts aesthetic, but social housing soon became a driving preoccupation for many of Modernism's early pioneers. Innovative technologies, a rational approach to planning, and new forms, they believed, would allow architectures to contribute to a reshaping of society. These concerns came to a head with the Weissenhof Estate in Stuttgart, a project organised in 1927 by the Deutscher Werkbund and overseen by Ludwig Mies van der Rohe, in which a star cast of architects presented 21 exemplary designs built as a showcase for social housing projects in the Modern style. Contributors included two architects whose designs of social housing were fundamental to the formulation of Modernism – JJP Oud and Le Corbusier.

The same year, another milestone in public housing began in Vienna. The Karl Marx Hof designed by Karl Ehn (who had studied with Adolf Loos) is a kilometre-long building that contains nearly 1,400 flats, most with balconies. It adopted a viaduct-like form with arches and two-tone colour scheme to soften the impact of its enormous size. The design took its inspiration from Socialist housing schemes of London rather than formal purity of Modernism, and its alternative approach to high-density housing has made it one of the most important and influential buildings of the century.

However it was the Modernist tradition, particularly as espoused by Le Corbusier in his epochal 1953 Unité d'Habitation in Marseilles, that dominated post-war social housing. Its model of towering blocks providing modular housing and incorporating various other social utilities was widely adopted as a low-cost solution to housing problems, though often poorly implemented and cheaply built.

By the 1970s, many post-war Modernist housing estates had become very unpopular and were blamed for causing social ills rather than solving them as originally intended. Many were torn down, and the destruction in 1972 of the once exemplary 1955 Pruitt-Igloe low-cost housing scheme designed by Minoru Yamasaki in St Louis, Missouri, has sometimes been presented as Modernism's death knell.

The disintegration of Modernism in the 1970s coincided with the waning of Socialism as a major political force in the West. The anti-welfare state policies pursued by Margaret Thatcher in the UK and Ronald Reagan in the US pushed social housing off the agenda in many countries, and those projects that went ahead did so with a renewed focus on traditional, single-unit housing.

Whereas once leading architects saw themselves tasked with creating solutions to wider public needs, now celebrity architects devoted themselves to

'Nothing is too good for ordinary people.'
Berthold Lubetkin

creating iconic cultural monuments or one-off luxury homes for the rich. When social housing is built, it has to be designed by lesser-known specialist architects. One of the few major contemporary practices of international renown that continues to show an interest in social housing is the innovative Danish outfit Bjarke Ingels Group, also known as BIG.

Arne Jacobsen

Denmark's most influential architect and designer, Arne Jacobsen, is best known for a string of important classic modern furniture designs and buildings that came to define a more discreet and regionally inflected form of post-war Modernism.

Born: 1902, Copenhagen, Denmark
Importance: Developed a characteristically Danish form of Modernism
Died: 1971, Copenhagen, Denmark

A contemporary of the great Finnish architect Alvar Aalto, Jacobsen similarly combined the innovations of the International Style with more local traditions, in particular the designs of Swedish architect Erik Gunnar Asplund, to create a distinctive Nordic design idiom.

His early works, such as his first major public commission, the Bellavista Housing Estate, in Klampenborg (1931–34), displayed a mastery of Modernism's fundamental tenets, but had yet to show the emergence of a distinctive voice. In contrast to Aalto, it is Jacobsen's post-war projects that are most significant. They are exemplary of the third-generation Modernism of the 1950s and 1960s that was less austere, more decorative and marked by a distinctive regional flavour.

Returning to Denmark after World War II (he had been forced to flee because of his Jewish ancestry), he built himself a deceptively simple yet widely admired brick house in 1947. Eschewing grand and flamboyant gestures to instead focus on incredibly fine detailing and simple, pared-down forms, it underpinned a style of Modern suburban housing that became very popular in the 1960s and 1970s across Northern Europe. This sensitive use of brick became a widely admired feature of his architecture.

Jacobsen's interest in detailing fed a passion for furniture design, inspired also by the example of the American husband-and-wife team of Charles and Ray Eames. The commission to design the SAS Royal

Hotel in Copenhagen (1957) was the ideal springboard for him to show off all his talents to create a *'The fundamental factor is proportion.'* total environment, famously designed right down to its doorknobs. The commercial form of the skyscraper was given a lighter touch for its new purpose as a hotel, with an especially delicate glass façade. For its lobby, Jacobsen designed the now iconic Egg and Swan chairs.

Even more obsessively detailed is St Catherine's College, Oxford (1963). Jacobsen insisted on a clause in his contract that would allow him to design everything from the gardens to the lampshades of this new student college. The buildings of St Catherine's, which have remained largely unchanged, are now seen as a paragon of the sensitive integration of Modern architectural forms and a garden environment.

Jacobsen's buildings are characterised by a lightness of touch and refined, distilled forms, with formal finesse as the guiding criterion. However, as important and beautiful as his buildings are, they will always be shaded by the success of his Ant and Egg chairs, which have become emblematic of post-war Modernism.

St Catherine's College, Oxford: Jacobsen also designed every interior feature.

Brazilian Modernist
Oscar Niemeyer

Modernism and the ideas of Le Corbusier were adopted around the world, but nowhere with more individuality and panache than by Oscar Niemeyer in Brazil. Exploiting the sculptural possibilities of reinforced concrete, the prolific Niemeyer has designed some of the most outlandish buildings of the 20th century.

Born: 1907, Rio de Janiero, Brazil
Importance:
Developed a distinctive and curvaceous Brazilian brand of Modernism

In 1936, Le Corbusier was invited to Brazil to design a building to house the Ministry of Health and Education. One of his collaborators on the ingeniously shuttered concrete high-rise was a local architect, Oscar Niemeyer.

Niemeyer took what he wanted from European Modernism, but was influenced, too, by the voluptuous legacy of Baroque architecture, creating a distinctive new language of Modernist architecture. Rather than the functional aspects prioritised

Niemeyer's Cathedral of Our Lady, Brasilia, is a giant crown of thorns.

by the Europeans, Niemeyer put the sensual and emotional centre stage. And while Modernist architecture had been characterised by the right angle and the cube, Niemeyer instead saw the possibilities of using reinforced concrete to create curvaceous and dramatic shapes. 'You always have the mountains of Rio in your eyes', Le Corbusier is reported to have told him.

This distinctive architecture is apparent in Niemeyer's first major work, the Church of St Francis in Pampulha, Brazil. Its undulating vaulted concrete roofs seem organic but rely on complex structural computations. With an invitation to collaborate with Le Corbusier on the United Nations headquarters in New York (1947), Niemeyer's international reputation was affirmed.

At home in Brazil, Niemeyer was invited to work on an audacious plan to build a new capital city, called Brasilia, from scratch on a new site in the middle of the country. Close associate Lucío Costa was responsible for the grand urban planning, but the new city's main buildings were designed in a theatrical yet monumental style by Niemeyer. For the National Congress Building, elemental forms were used on a gigantic scale to impressive effect, while the Presidential Palace features unusually voluptuous upturned arches.

In its scope, Brasilia surpasses all other Modernist architectural projects, putting into reality ideas that had previously existed only in utopian sketches. Although they were subsequently seen as emblematic of the arrogance and failure of Modernism, Brasilia's grand architectural gestures and novel cityscape have again come into fashion.

A life-long Communist, Niemeyer was forced into exile during the fascist dictatorship in 1964, returning to Brazil 20 years later as democracy was re-established. Most notable of his later projects is the Niterói Contemporary Art Museum (1996), which sits like a UFO on the hills of Rio. Niemeyer's work introduced Modernism to Latin America and then continued to dominate it for decade after decade. Adored and reviled in equal measure, his buildings showed the way to Modernism's lighter side.

Kenzo Tange

One of the most revered architects of the latter 20th century, Kenzo Tange combined lessons drawn from Le Corbusier with traditional Japanese sensibilities to develop a new subtle, regionally inflected kind of Modernism. His buildings, often praised for their remarkable beauty, were instrumental in projecting the new face of post-war Japan.

Born: 1913, Imabari, Japan
Importance: Designer of post-war Japan's most iconic buildings
Died: 2005, Tokyo, Japan

As a student, Tange venerated Le Corbusier, studying with one of his favoured pupils, Kunio Mayekawa. He established the Tange Laboratory, many students of which went on to become famous in their own right, and took up a teaching post at the Tokyo University.

In 1949, Tange was commissioned to design the Hiroshima Peace Memorial, a building of huge symbolic importance both nationally and internationally. Tange responded with a restrained building, whose rectilinear shape, pilotis and concrete adhered to Corbusian orthodoxy but expressed with a delicate refinement which was unmistakeably Japanese in character.

Throughout his career, Tange spoke about the difficulties of reconciling traditional and contemporary forms, something that his buildings, however, usually accomplished in exemplary fashion. He was equally keen that his design philosophy should not stagnate and should develop with each successive project.

As interested in urban planning as architecture, Tange published *A Plan for Tokyo* in 1960. His proposal was for a 'metabolist' scheme that would house 25,000 in modular structures supported on columns over the water of Tokyo Bay. While the grandiose plan was not implemented, it is widely acknowledged as one of the most visionary and studied of 20th-century urban planning designs.

Its modular design philosophy did, however, influence the 1967 Yamanashi Press and Broadcast Centre in Kofu, in which the working areas seem like interchangeable blocks supported by a series of circular towers.

Completely different in nature are two of his best-loved designs, both in Tokyo – St Mary's Cathedral and the buildings for the 1964 Olympics. The cathedral's soaring concrete walls create the shape of the cross and remain true to Tange's aspirations of interpreting traditional architecture through the lens of Modernism. Fittingly, the cathedral served as the location of his funeral when he died in 2005 at the age of 91.

In his design of the National Stadium for the 1964 Olympics in Tokyo, Tange sought to give concrete expression to Japan's rising industrial prowess yet maintain a sense of refined delicacy. Its steel roof, descending like a spiral from a central tower, supported descriptions of his work as 'structural expressionist', and its dynamic shape was admired by millions of people around the world, cementing his international stature.

Tange continued to practice into his late 80s, becoming an emblem of Modern Japan and establishing in the process a tradition of Japanese contemporary architecture that continues to be held in the highest regard.

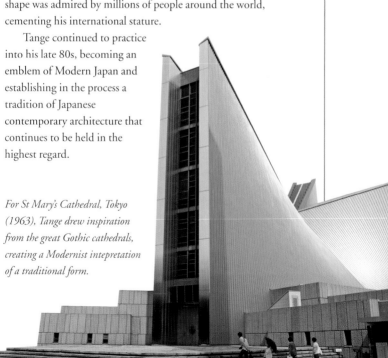

For St Mary's Cathedral, Tokyo (1963), Tange drew inspiration from the great Gothic cathedrals, creating a Modernist intepretation of a traditional form.

Eero Saarinen

Known equally for his furniture and architecture, Finnish-American Eero Saarinen developed Modernism in various directions that became characteristic of the optimism of post-war America. His works contributed to the popularisation of Modernism and its adoption into the mainstream of American design.

Born: 1910, Kirkkonummi, Finland
Importance: Designer of important eclectic and sculptural buildings in the United States
Died: 1961, Ann Arbor, Michigan, United States

Saarinen was born into architecture; his father Eliel was a significant architect in his own right, designing important buildings such as Helsinki Station (1914). In 1923, the Saarinen family emigrated to the United States, where Eero studied architecture and became a naturalised citizen in 1940. During his studies he associated closely with other seminal mid-century Modernists, including Charles and Ray Eames.

Saarinen went into practice with his father, and like him, developed a pragmatic ability to adapt various contrasting architectural idioms according to the nature of the commission rather than adhere to one dogmatic approach or develop a consistent, readily identifiable style.

The General Motors Technical Center in Detroit (1951) was a widely admired steel-and-glass corporate structure, whose purity and refined detail would have been impossible without the previous example of Ludwig Mies van der Rohe. The sculptural qualities of two separate features – an aluminium-clad dome and a water tower – however, hint at future directions in Saarinen's architecture.

Saarinen's most famous building could not be further from the

'We wanted passengers passing through the building to experience a fully-designed environment.'

anonymous perfection of the General Motors Technical Center. Begun in 1956 and completed in 1961, the TWA terminal at John F Kennedy International Airport in New York is a voluptuous and expressionist assemblage of curvaceous forms seemingly made of plasticine rather than concrete.

The terminal is the architectural equivalent of the flamboyant, futuristic styling of American consumer products and cars of the late 1950s. It encapsulated the glamour of flying, as did the swooping lines of Washington Dulles International Airport, Virginia, designed in 1958. But the freely drawn nature of these airports and their apparent carefree abandon alarmed and confused critics, particularly given their inconsistency with his previous work.

The airport buildings' expressionist bent is picked up in the iconic Gateway Arch in St Louis, which was completed posthumously in 1965. Celebrating America's expansion west, it is a simple yet enormous (192m/630ft) arch that cleverly frames various sightlines around the city.

TWA Terminal at John F Kennedy International Airport, New York.

Saarinen is as well known for his organic furniture designs as his buildings, in particular the Tulip Chair and Table he designed for the Knoll furniture firm. Some of the sensibility rubbed off on his architectural practice, in particular his penchant for creating large-scale working models of buildings during the design process.

Saarinen's early death of a heart attack robbed America of one of its most creative architects. Nine major projects he had on the drawing board at the time of his death were finished posthumously.

Jørn Oberg Utzon

Few architects are as associated with a single building to the extent that Danish architect Jørn Utzon, designer of Sydney Opera House, is. Undisputedly one of the 20th century's most important monuments, it is also the only structure to have been made a World Heritage Site during the life of its creator.

Born: 1918, Aalberg, Denmark
Importance: Designer of the iconic Sydney Opera House
Died: 2008, Majorca, Spain

Utzon studied with seminal Scandivanian Modernists Alvar Aalto and Erik Gunnar Asplund, and was as interested in the work of Frank Lloyd Wright as he was by that of the standard bearers of High Modernism. Utzon also professed a deep admiration for structures of other cultures, including Chinese, Mayan and Islamic, which lent his structures a wider formal vocabulary.

Sydney Opera House became a World Heritage Site in 2007.

Utzon had the gift of creating unusual architectural forms that were also popular with the public. Building on advances in construction technology, he was able to use concrete in a particularly free way to create complex forms and curves. And rather than the flat roof that was a cardinal feature of Modernist architecture, Utzon preferred roofs that were pitched, often dramatically, a feature that was to define his most famous building.

Even though he was a little-known architect, his unusual entry to the international competition to build the Sydney Opera House caught the eye of one of the judges, Finnish architect Eero Saarinen, who then pressed for it to be made the winner. Despite its status today as one of the best-known buildings in the world and emblem of modern Australia, the construction of the Sydney Opera House was tortuous and controversial, lasting from 1959 to 1973.

Inspired by the wings of a bird, the building's enormous 60m (197ft) concrete shell vaults pushed structural engineering technology to its limit and led to serious arguments with compatriot Ove Arup, one of the most famous structural engineers of the century, who joined him on the project. The difficulty and expense of the build led to increasing hostility from politicians and, eventually, Utzon was sacked from his own project. He was not present at the building's opening and never saw the completed structure in the flesh. Despite being treated poorly by the city he helped put on the international map, architects and critics around the world were stunned by the building's originality, which initiated several major commissions.

Most notable of these are the Bagsværd Church, a delicate glass-roofed church near Copenhagen, and the canopy-like structure he designed for the Kuwait National Assembly. Despite being made of concrete, its open forms seem soft, convincingly emulating the billowing fabric of a Bedouin tent. Nevertheless, the Sydney Opera House towers above his other achievements. It altered perceptions of modern Australia and changed the practice of architecture as the race to develop iconic structures overtook the purist principles of Modernism.

Richard Neutra

Richard Neutra brought High Modernism to California, adapting it to the West Coast climate and lifestyle to create elegant breezy homes that integrated the exterior landscape with clean-lined interiors. Often designed for celebrities, Neutra's villas have come to typify the glamour of mid-century California.

Born: 1892, Vienna, Austria
Importance: Created Modernist buildings that defined mid-century California
Died: 1970, Wuppertal, Germany

Born in Vienna, Neutra formed part of the mass migration to the United States of some of Central Europe's most creative and innovative minds. His education reads like a roll call of some of the century's most famous architects: he studied and worked in the studios of Otto Wagner, Adolf Loos, Erich Mendelsohn and Frank Lloyd Wright. While many European architects headed for the East Coast, Neutra accepted an invitation to join fellow Austrian émigré Rudolf Schindler in Los Angeles.

Setting up in practice on his own, Neutra specialised in domestic architecture, to which he brought the geometric, rectilinear language of the International Style with its flat roofs and curtain walls. Neutra adapted this vocabulary to create buildings that suited the needs of his often very wealthy clients and that would integrate with the surrounding landscape. The clean, 'hygienic' lines and large glass expanses characteristic of his style were already in evidence in one of his earliest and most admired villas, the Lovell House, completed in 1929. The building is also historically important for its introduction of the construction techniques of commercial architecture, such as steel structures and sprayed concrete, to residential projects.

Considered one of the most accomplished and important residential designs of the 20th century, Kaufman House (1946) was commissioned by the same far-sighted business tycoon, Erich

Kaufman House (1946), Neutra's widely acknowledged masterpiece.

Kaufman, who a decade earlier had commissioned another of the most important homes of the century, Frank Lloyd Wright's Fallingwater. Like Wright, Neutra produced a design that integrated with its landscape in exemplary fashion, this time the desert of Palm Springs rather than Pennsylvanian forest. Neutra's design employs simple low volumes and glass walls that open onto patios that merge with the swimming pool and desert landscape, creating luxury and glamour with an impressive economy of means.

The recent rehabilitation of mid-century Modernism has led to a resurgence of interest in Neutra's buildings, which have been transformed from dated structures to become the epitome of cool. Featuring in Hollywood films and glossy magazines, Neutra's houses, with their breezy elegance, are once again influencing new residential building in California. This rediscovered appreciation for his work has not been enough to stop the destruction of his buildings, however: one of his houses in Palm Springs was demolished as recently as 2002.

Founders of Prefabrication in Architecture

Charles and Ray Eames

One of the most renowned husband and wife teams of the 20th century, Charles and Ray Eames are particularly revered for some of the most distinctive and popular furniture designs of all time, and applied the same creative intelligence to a variety of other fields, including architecture. Their own house is one of the seminal homes of the 20th century and one of the most admired examples of prefabrication in architecture.

Born: (Charles Eames) 1907, St Louis, Missouri, United States; (Ray Eames) 1912, Sacramento, California, United States

Importance: Exemplary use of prefabrication in architecture

Died: (Charles) 1978, St Louis, Missouri, United States; (Ray) 1988, Los Angeles, California, United States

The Eames House was commissioned as one of the famous Case Study Houses, the brainchild of John Entenza, the influential and enlightened editor of the magazine *Arts &Architecture*, who was instrumental in popularising Modernist architecture and the art of contemporary artists such as Jackson Pollock and Mark Rothko.

The aim of these seminal houses was to showcase the benefits of Modernist design principles and how they could result in homes superior to those executed to conventional and traditional designs. The entire process of their design and construction was meticulously documented and published, and many important mid-century architects were involved, including Eero Saarinen, Richard Neutra, Pierre Koenig and Raphael Soriano.

The Eames had already collaborated with a friend of theirs, the Finnish-American architect Eero Saarinen, on an earlier Case Study House intended as a home for Entenza himself. But for their own home, they developed an even more original glass shed-like structure. Its completion was delayed by the post-war shortage of steel, and the structure was finally finished in 1949, after a very short build.

Situated between steep banking and a glade of trees, it used standard off-the-peg factory components for its slim steel framing and glass panelling. The use of primary colours for some of the panels evokes the style of De Stijl, while the delicacy of its walls references traditional Japanese architecture. The house is on two storeys, and the airy living room is treated to a double-height space and glass front, shielded on one side by characteristic wood panelling.

Like the Eames's furniture, the house manages to take the features of High Modernism and yet deliver them in a manner that is appealing and welcoming, in contrast to the occasional severe austerity of Modernism's great European practitioners. The Eames House was comfortable enough to serve as the couple's home until their death and is now preserved in the form that it was left as a monument to their life and designs.

The Eames House remains an important example of an alternative type of architectural process, with its ingenious application of design-led problem solving contrasting with the grander theoretical approach of contemporaneous architects. A recent resurgence in interest in prefabrication as well as a popularising of the design language of the 1950s (due in no small part to the Eames' own furniture) has made the Eames House once again an object of study.

Eames House, designed as part of the seminal Case Study Houses project (1949).

Richard Meier

Richard Meier is an important American Neo- Modernist architect, famed for his large museum projects, notably the Getty Centre, and instantly recognisable white, chaste, formal language. He was particularly prominent in the 1980s, when he was the youngest ever recipient of the Pritzker Prize, architecture's highest award.

Born: 1934, Newark, New Jersey, United States

Importance: Influential Neo-Modernist known in particular for his museum designs

Meier was one of the New York Five, a group of emerging architects identified by Arthur Drexler for an important exhibition in 1967 at the Museum of Modern Art in New York City. While the five architects (also including Peter Eisenman, Michael Graves, Charles Gwathmey and John Hejduk) had little more in common than an engagement with the legacy of Modernism, the exhibition and accompanying book made each of them well known. Each in his own way sought to rescue the early, pure formal expression of Modernism exemplified by Le Corbusier's Purist villas and Gerrit Rietveld's Schröder House and find ways of using them in a contemporary context.

Meier was, however, the only one of the five to stay true to this admiring recapitulation of Modernism. He used the identifying features of early Modernism, such as the white-washed geometric wall and the curved handrail or staircase, but reconfigured them out of context to create his own distinctive formal language. Like the others in the New York Five, Meier was largely uninterested in the philosophical and political underpinnings of Modernism, looking instead to exploit its sculptural and aesthetic features to create pleasurable and beautiful contemporary spaces. As such, Meier's architecture can be seen to have much in common with Minimalist artists such as Donald Judd, who were attempting to reduce Modernism right down to its essential visual building blocks.

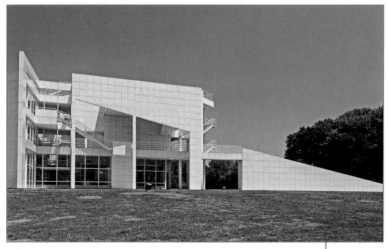

The Atheneum Visitor Center, New Harmony, Indiana, United States (1979).

Meier emphasised the important of natural light in his designs, a concern already evident in his first major commission, the Smith House in Connecticut, designed in 1965.

The Atheneum Visitor Centre, completed in 1979 in the historic town of New Harmony, Indiana, is perhaps one of his most successful public buildings in its reconfiguration of Modernism. It was one in a string of important museum and gallery commissions, including the Arp Museum (1978) and Frankfurt Museum of Applied Art (1979) in Germany, the Museum of Contemporary Art, Barcelona (1987) and the Museum of Television & Radio in Beverly Hills. His most significant commission was the Getty Center in California, but its completion in 1997 was greeted with mixed reviews.

Meier's designs have remained remarkably consistent from the beginning of his career to the present, which has resulted in his work moving in and out of vogue. His gleaming white buildings have also set an important precedent for more recent Minimalist architects.

> **NEO-MODERNISM**
> In architecture, Neo-Modernism describes the return in the 1990s to the stricter formal language of Modernism after the radical and playful eclecticism of Post-Modernism. It is characterised by the use of steel and glass.

Richard Rogers

Richard Rogers, along with Norman Foster and James Stirling, put modern British architecture on the global map. His exuberant version of the High Tech style has resulted in some of the most iconic and popular buildings of the last decades and made him hugely popular.

Born: 1933, Florence, Italy
Importance: Pioneer of the High Tech style

Rogers studied in Britain and the United States before going into practice first with Norman Foster and then with Italian architect Renzo Piano. In 1971, he and structural engineer Peter Rice won the competition to design the Pompidou Centre in Paris with an outlandish design. All the service ducts and piping were placed on the exterior of the building like spaghetti and the lifts and elevators put in transparent tubes. The building was greeted with astonishment when it was finished in 1976 and has since become a major tourist destination. It

remains the most important, and best-loved, example of the High Tech movement in architecture (also known as Structural Expressionism) that developed in response to the decline of Modernism.

In practice on his own, Roger's next major project was the Lloyds Building in London, completed in 1984, which, like the

The Pompidou Centre is now a major Paris tourist attraction.

Pompidou Centre, was designed inside-out, with all its services exteriorised to striking ornamental effect. This aspect of Roger's buildings has also led to their designation as 'Bowellist'.

'Technology cannot be an end in itself but must aim at solving long term social and ecological problems.'

The flamboyant and very contemporary nature of his designs put Rogers on a highly publicised collision course with architectural conservatives, most notably an ongoing spat with Prince Charles, who famously criticised his (unbuilt) design for an extension to the National Gallery in London as a 'monstrous carbuncle'. Such controversy did little to stop Rogers being considered one of the most important architects of his time and large commissions come flooding in from around the world.

Two significant examples of recent work are the Millennium Dome (1999) in London, whose architectural quality was overshadowed by politics and the lack of a coherent vision for its use, and Terminal 4 of Barajas Airport in Madrid (2005), which features a softly undulating roof and uses bright colours to create an unusually friendly and relaxing environment that exemplifies the increasingly humanist and ecological bent of his designs.

The Richard Rogers Partnership renamed itself Rogers Stirk Harbour + Partners in 2007 and remains one of the largest and most important current architectural practices. Like that of his former colleague Norman Foster, Roger's work has outlasted the approach of contemporary Post-Modernism and has come to define a technological style of British architecture that has become globally dominant.

HIGH TECH
This form of Structural Expressionism was prominent in the 1970s and 80s. No longer hidden away, the new technological elements of building were put on display, and structural and service elements, such as piping, exposed for decorative effect.

Norman Foster

One of the most accomplished architects of his generation, Norman Foster is known for designs that display technological mastery coupled with supreme detailing. In Foster's hands, the Modernist materials of steel and glass have been given a new lease of life and used with a virtuosity previously impossible.

Born: 1935, Manchester, England
Importance: Leading Neo-Modernist architect

Foster studied alongside Richard Rogers, with whom he also was initially in practice. While Rogers developed the High Tech style in a flamboyant and playful direction, however, Foster used it to create a variety of more austere and elegant structures whose subtlety of detailing places him in the tradition of Modernist maestros Ludwig Mies van der Rohe and Arne Jacobsen. But beneath their surface perfection, his designs are marked by ingenuity (for instance, economy of construction or prefabrication), and he has shown an ability to completely rethink a given category, most notably the airport and the skyscraper.

The curved forms of 30 St Mary Axe (2004), the London skyscraper known as 'The Gherkin', have made it one of the world's most famous buildings. But its form is not gratuitous – the shape minimises wind loads and allows the management of convection currents within the building to reduce heating requirements. These green concerns were prefigured by the Commerzbank Tower in Frankfurt (1997), which, as well as being Europe's tallest building at the time, also featured an array of innovative ecological technologies.

The Gherkin's formal ingenuity was pre-shadowed by the Hong Kong and Shanghai Bank (HSBC Main Building), completed in 1986. Constructed at enormous cost, it was one of the most admired buildings of its time. It features a steel exoskeleton, inside of which the modular and flexible office spaces of the skyscraper seem to be hung.

Foster claims, with some justification, to have reconsidered airport design by proceeding from first principles. Stansted Airport (1991), London's third airport, confounded precedent by creating a simple upside-down building in which all the services are hidden beneath a large light shed-like structure that evokes Victorian train stations with its dappled natural light. This simple, airy approach to the airport interior was developed on a much larger scale for Hong Kong's new airport Chek Lap Kok (1998). An impressive and extremely complex project, the airport is shaped like a bird and built on reclaimed land.

While large corporate structures have come to dominate Foster's output, he has continued to design diverse projects, including the impressive Millau Viaduct (2004) in Southern France, the highest and one of the longest bridges in the world, whose subtle and elegant geometry integrates beautifully with the valley it spans.

As one of the largest practices in the world, with offices in 20 countries, the influence of Foster + Partners on the global landscape is considerable. However, in its dominance, the glass-and-steel corporate look of the enormous number of buildings designed by his practice has perhaps become over-common and almost generic.

30 St Mary Axe, London (2004), more commonly known as 'The Gherkin' because of its shape.

Kisho Kurokawa

Widely acclaimed Japanese architect Kisho Kurokawa has moved away from the functionalist machine aesthetics of international Modernism to create subtle and ambiguous buildings informed by traditional Japanese notions of space. As well as designing masterful buildings, Kurokawa is known for his philosophical works, which are deeply influenced by Buddhism.

Born: 1934, Nagoya, Japan
Importance: Leading proponent of the Japanese Metabolist Movement and later 'symbiotic' architecture
Died: 2007, Tokyo, Japan

Kurokawa, who studied with Kenzo Tange, expressed shock at the way that the machine aesthetics propagated by Le Corbusier were being uncritically imported, including by his teacher. This critique of Western architecture resulted in the important 1959 essay 'From the Age of the Machine to the Age of Life', which was later also the subject of a major travelling international exhibition.

Kurokawa sprang to prominence at the age of 26 as the leading figure of the Metabolist Movement. This was an avant-garde grouping formed in 1960 around the radical idea that buildings could be decentralised and modular, growing organically like natural phenomena. It had many elements in common with the entirely separate and equally influential Archigram group that was concurrent in London.

The Nakagin Capsule Tower is the most famous example of this trend. A series of small concrete blocks containing tiny cheap overnight hotel rooms are assembled like blocks of Lego. The futuristic structure gave the appearance of being flexible, seemingly allowing the more self-sufficient 'pods' to be added or exchanged as required.

As Kurokawa's philosophical interest in Buddhism developed, he began to focus instead on 'symbiotic' architecture. This investigated the relation between the public and the private spheres (exemplified by the porch, or Japanese *engawa*), the use of local materials and avoidance of bright colours, and the possibility of creating ambiguous spaces that would welcome both pleasure and reflection.

Kuala Lumpur International Airport, completed in 1998, is the masterpiece of this later direction, lauded for its integration of an enormous five-runway airport with the tropical forest in which it is located. Symbiotic principles were expressed not only through integration with surrounding vegetation, but culturally – Kurokawa employed forms that evoked traditional Islamic culture. The National Art Centre in Tokyo, completed in 2006, also exemplifies his theoretical approach to architecture. It has a deliberately ambiguous wavy glass façade, which Kurokawa himself has described as 'fuzzy'.

By the time of his death, Kurokawa presided over a large office designing major projects around the world. He was an important figure in Japan: married to a famous actress and friend of leading politicians and celebrities, he also ran a (failed) bid to become a governor of Tokyo.

Many of Kurokawa's interests, such as ecology, respect for nature and reuse, which seemed esoteric when first espoused, have been at least partially adopted in the architectural mainstream. His earlier modular buildings were also very influential, particularly on the High Tech style practised by architects including Renzo Piano and Richard Roger.

Nakagin Capsule Tower (1972), the most important example of Japanese Metabolist architecture.

Jean Nouvel

**Prolific French architect Jean Nouvel has established an
international reputation as one of the leading contemporary
architects as a result of a succession of highly imaginative and
iconoclastic buildings. Defying easy categorisation,
his designs often feature a flamboyant yet
undogmatic use of technology and extrovert
use of colour.**

Born: 1945, Fumel,
France
Importance:
Iconoclastic
contemporary architect
of great originality

Like many other architects before him, Nouvel is best
known for his first major commission, the Institut du
Monde Arabe (Arab World Institute). This was one of
French president François Mitterrand's famous 'Grand
Projets', a series of commissions of iconic buildings
intended to overhaul the image of Paris. Nouvel's design, completed
in 1987, was quite unlike anything else, and immediately established
him as one of architecture's superstars.

For the building's stunning south façade, Nouvel reinterpreted
traditional Arabic *mashrabiya* wooden screens in technological terms,
with intricate metal shutters controlled individually by electronic
servers continually shifting to adopt different patterns and to control
the amount of light admitted into the building. The building has
become a Paris landmark, and exemplifies a characteristic of Nouvel's
otherwise heterogeneous buildings: they appear modern without,
however, having recourse to the formal vocabulary or theoretical
underpinnings of either Modernism or Post-Modernism.

For his 2005 Torre Agbar skyscraper in Barcelona, Nouvel
adopted a similar cylindrical form to Norman Foster's contemporaneous
30 St Mary Axe. But instead of the austere materials and formal
discipline that mark the London building, Nouvel's structure is a riot
of colour. His Tour de Verre, an all-glass tapering skyscraper designed

Institut du Monde Arabe (Arab World Institute), Paris (1980).

for New York City, but awaiting planning permission, promises to be one of the most exciting skyscrapers the city has seen for some time.

Nouvel is particularly known for a series of major cultural buildings. The 2006 Quai Branly Museum in Paris is made of red blocks that snake around a plan following the path of the neighbouring river Seine, while the Guthrie Theatre in Minneapolis, completed in the same year, is an assemblage of shiny black box-like volumes on which photographs are projected. The earlier Fondation Cartier pour l'Art Contemporain in Paris, completed in 1994, is widely appreciated for its more subtle qualities. It is a light and ethereal structure made predominately of glass, which ingratiates itself with natural features by incorporating pre-existing trees into the design.

Nouvel is in high demand, and his large studio is executing designs for some of the most significant commissions around the world. Awarding him the prestigious Pritzker Prize in 2008, the jury praised him for 'greatly expanding the vocabulary of contemporary architecture'. While his highly original buildings have acted as a foil to the drab conformity of much contemporary architecture, the cult of the 'starchitect' now appears to be on the wane in favour of less authorial and splashy design philosophies.

Frank Gehry

A popular contemporary architect, Frank Gehry has a stellar profile following the incredible success of his outlandish shiny Guggenheim Museum in Bilbao. He has been associated with the Deconstructivist trend in architecture and has come under sustained criticism from his peers.

Born: 1929, Toronto, Canada
Importance: Controversial designer of Deconstructivist buildings

Gehry's designs are typified by their sense of humour, a quality shared by some Post-Modernist contemporaries, but expressed by Gehry without heaviness or Classicist references, features he has publicly mocked. For the 1984 California Aerospace Museum, an early commission completed for the Los Angeles Olympics, for instance, he perched a decommissioned fighter jet on the façade, creating an effect that was more surreal than kitsch.

He had previously been known in architectural circles primarily for his theoretical 'paper architecture', and for his own extraordinary house in Santa Monica, in which he made a series of additions to a normal suburban house using a jumble of plywood and corrugated iron. The resultant assemblage, which avoided any sort of regular geometry, seemed fragmentary and provisional, and established a chaotic formal language that he was to employ on future projects.

Vitra, a major Swiss furniture company, commissioned Gehry to design its museum in Weil-am-Rhein in Germany. Completed in 1988, its crazy and eccentric sculptural forms poked fun at architectural convention, but also led to a series of commissions for similar designs. Most notable was the commission of his masterpiece, the Guggenheim Museum in the then forlorn industrial city of Bilbao in northern Spain. Famously inspired by fish, he created even more outlandish shapes and swirls, clad this time in titanium 'scales' that glinted and reflected in the light. It single-handedly transformed

Bilbao into a major tourist destination over night. The Walt Disney Concert Hall in Los Angeles employs a similar chaotic formal language, this time using sails as a reference for its swooping, metallic exterior.

These tilting wayward forms also feature in domestic projects, notably the surreal Schnabel House, in Brentwood, California (1990). A gentler, less self-indulgent aspect to his design is evident in the 2003 Maggie's Centre, a cancer respite centre in Dundee, Scotland.

While Gehry is one of the few contemporary architects who can properly be described as a household name, his work has stoked considerable controversy in architectural circles. His detractors often argue his work is frivolously iconic, repetitious, or conceived solely as an attention-grabbing exterior form with little consideration for its use or interior. Nevertheless, his Guggenheim Museum remains incontrovertibly one of the buildings of the century and his style is as inimitable as that of Gaudí.

DECONSTRUCTIVISM
Starting in the 1970s, Deconstructivist architects began to dismantle the expected vocabulary of building to create unexpected, unpredictable and fragmentary forms. Deconstructivism takes an irrational approach to design and is influenced by contemporaneous Post-Modern philosophy.

Walt Disney Concert Hall, Los Angeles (2003).

Robert Venturi

One of the most dominant figures in post-war architecture, Robert Venturi has been prominent as an academic and theorist as well as an architect in his own right. His diverse output is usually seen as Post-Modernist, a description that he himself rejects.

Born: 1935, Philadelphia, Pennsylvania, United States

Importance: Leading architectural critic and influential Post-Modernist architect

After working in the offices of Eero Saarinen and Louis Kahn, Venturi established himself primarily as an academic. His 1966 *Complexity and Contradiction in Architecture*, the first in a string of groundbreaking books, was influential for its radical challenge of Modernist orthodoxy. He called for 'an architecture that promotes richness and ambiguity over unity and clarity, contradiction and redundancy over harmony and simplicity.'

It famously mocks Ludwig Mies van der Rohe's dictum 'less is more' with the retort 'less is bore'. Even though he professed a deep admiration for seminal Modernists Le Corbusier and Alvar Aalto, he became a lightening rod for dissent and the emerging Post-Modernists. Venturi, though, has maintained he was only criticising bland and sloppy later expressions of Modernism.

Learning from Las Vegas, published in 1972, was even more controversial. It is one of the most important texts of Post-Modernism and cultural theory of the latter 20th century. Outlining an ironic stance of appreciation of the high capitalist kitsch of Las Vegas as an act of sympathy for the taste of the common man, it managed to recuperate a whole swathe of artefacts for cultural rehabilitation in film, music and photography as well as architecture and design.

Venturi's best-known building, Vanna Venturi House (1963), dates from the beginning of his career and is often presented as the first Post-Modern design. It reconfigures various traditional elements,

Vanna Venturi House, the house Venturi designed for his mother in 1963.

such as mouldings, gables and a pitched roof, which would have been anathema to Modernists, to create a striking home.

In 1969, he was joined in practice by his wife Denise Scott Brown, and established a Philadelphia-based practice responsible for a number of significant commissions, particularly during the 1970s, that continues today as Venturi Scott Brown and Associates.

In 1991, he was selected to design the Sainsbury Wing extension to the National Gallery in London, following a furious controversy initiated by the intervention of Prince Charles. The innocuous and cautious stone-clad building that resulted has often been seen since as a missed opportunity and criticised as pastiche. The same year, Venturi was awarded the Pritzker Prize, its jury singling out how he diverted 'the mainstream of architecture away from Modernism'.

In his creation of a culture of ironic eclecticism, Venturi's cultural influence extends well beyond the field of architecture. Within architecture itself – and despite his own protestations – he is seen as having dealt Modernism its hammer blow, providing the theoretical underpinnings for the various architectural strands that emerged from under its shadows.

POST-MODERNISM

So overwhelming was the influence of Modernism – and Le Corbusier in particular – on architects, that it was only in the 1970s that leading architects began to seriously challenge some of its main assumptions.

If Modernism was tied up with utopian beliefs, often linked to Communism, about progress and the ability of technology to improve lives, Post-Modernism took a more cynical and pessimistic view of the world. It saw the world as fractured, and believed no single narrative could dominate. Architecturally, this allowed the return of traditional forms, something that was seen both as provocative and very conservative.

One of the most famous examples of Post-Modernism is a skyscraper in New York City, designed by American architect Philip Johnson (who had previously been an influential Modernist) with John Burgee. The AT&T Building (completed in 1984 and now known as the Sony Building) is infamous for having a Neo-Georgian pediment at its top, which has led to it being referred to as the Chippendale-Highboy. The introduction of elements normally derided as kitsch and shared with low-grade suburban pastiche architecture caused fierce debate and opposition.

Another seminal Post-Modernist building was the Neue Staatsgalerie in Stuttgart, designed by British architect James Stirling and also completed in 1984. Its return to shapes and forms associated with the architecture of Ancient Greece, along with the introduction of luridly coloured elements, such as shocking pink handrails, made it a quintessential expression of the Post-Modernist style.

Post-Modernism was at its height in the late 1980s, and shared many of the same preoccupations as the reactionary politics of Ronald Reagan in the United States and Margaret Thatcher in Britain. As

1960s social housing was being torn down, it seemed that Modernism had run its course. The grandiose housing schemes of Modernism were now replaced by new smaller projects influenced by Post-Modernism, which were often much more traditional in scope.

Post-Modernism was a wider movement, not restricted to architecture. In fact, one of its most influential and famous manifestations was in the Memphis group headed up by legendary Austrian–Italian industrial designer Ettore Sottsass. The group's furniture, with its jarring colours and surprising reuse of traditional forms, proved very influential for other Post-Modernists, including architects. Post-Modernism was also closely paired with the philosophical movements of Deconstructivism and Post-Structuralism that dominated many university departments until the end of the 1990s.

The Post-Modernist movement is very much associated with the architectural critic Charles Jencks, who has returned to the subject again and again in his widely disseminated books, modifying his arguments and definitions of Post-Modernism each time. It remains a matter of critical debate as to whether certain important building, such as Richard Rogers's Lloyds Building, should be termed as Post-Modern or not. As a movement, Post-Modernism has currently fallen into disrepute, its buildings often seen as superficial, lacking in vigour and pretentious, and 'Po Mo' is now often used as a pejorative term by architects and critics.

> *'While once there were laws governing architectural grammar … nowadays there is only confusion and disagreement'*
>
> Charles Jencks

Michael Graves

Michael Graves is a prolific and controversial American architect who is best known for a series of seminal yet provocative designs in the 1980s that established Post-Modernism as a major, if controversial, presence in international architecture.

Born: 1934, Indianapolis, Indiana, United States
Importance: Leading American Post-Modernist

Like Richard Meier, Graves was initially one of the New York Five. However, he soon put the obsession with Corbusian forms evident in the 1969 Benacerraf House in Princeton behind him to become one of the most important protagonists of Post-Modernism. He began to incorporate elements drawn from his study of Renaissance architecture in Italy and other neglected architectural traditions into his work in a seemingly wilful fashion.

The Portland Public Services Building, completed in 1982, was a milestone in the development of Post-Modernism, and made the covers of both *Time* and *Newsweek* magazines. Its squat proportions and tiny windows, use of flashy colours and an array of arbitrary decorative elements, including a garland of blue ribbons (actually

'If I have a style, I am not aware of it.'

made of concrete), caused a sensation. While important historically, the building has not been a success with either critics or its users.

However, Graves's collaborations with Italian design groups Alessi and Memphis in the early 1980s were enormously successful, and his pyramid-shaped kettle for Alessi made him a household name.

The Humana Building, a skyscraper in Louisville, Kentucky, typically assembled a variety of self-conscious 'Classical' architectural references to mould an eccentric building, whose heavy use of marble evoked the monumental structures of Fascist Italy and Nazi Germany.

Most provocative of all his work are perhaps the series of buildings he designed for the Disney Corporation, which have been described as 'kitsch' by influential critic Charles Jencks. The Team Disney Building in Burbank, California (1991) features seven dwarves holding up the triangular Greek-inspired façade pediment, while the two Orlando Hotels are even more frivolous. The Dolphin Hotel adopts the shape of a giant pyramid, topped by two giant 17m (56ft) dolphin statues, while its sister building is crowned by two swan statues of similar size. The two buildings, completed in 1990, are separated by a large nine-storey-high water feature that evokes the grottos and fountains of Baroque Rome, reinterpreting them for the glitz of Florida.

Graves's controversial and largely unpopular Portland Public Services Building (1982).

Graves continues to oversee two large practices, one devoted to architecture and interior design, the other to product design and graphics, and still adheres in the historicist style of Post-Modernism.

While Graves's reputation, like that of Post-Modernism as a whole, may currently be residing in the doldrums, no account of the architectural history of the end of the 20th century would be complete without his distinctive creations. His use of traditional elements has been popular with cultural conservatives, and fuelled a resurgence of Neo-Classical motifs in American civic and residential architecture.

Toyo Ito

Cult Japanese architect Toyo Ito is revered by his peers for his shifting yet radically conceptual positions on the built environment and for a handful of ethereal, transparent structures. His uncompromising and rarified approach has led to relatively few of his designs being realised, which means he does not enjoy the popular profile of many of his contemporaries.

Born: 1941, Seoul, South Korea
Importance: Conceptual architect who has been as influential for his ideas as his buildings

Ito began his career in architecture working in the studio of Kiyonori Kikutake, one of the leading members of the Metabolist Movement, who believed in the social transformation that a genuinely modular architecture could effect. As the movement petered out and its aims seemed hopelessly optimistic, Ito turned in disillusion to a completely different kind of architecture in his own practice, creating buildings of the most self-effacing and modest kind.

He established his studio Urbot ('Urban Robot') in 1971, changing its name eight years later to the more conventional Toyo Ito & Associates, Architects. He initially worked on a variety of understated residential buildings, including the widely admired White U house. Designed in 1975 for his sister, it is a building of the utmost modesty and interiority. Consisting of a single-storey concrete U, its minimal interior looks solely onto the central courtyard, almost as if to shield itself from the outside world.

Ito modified this extreme approach to develop an architecture of transparency

'Whether in buildings or in cities, we walk through realms where symbols are drifting about and with these we weave the space of our own significance.'

and weightlessness. These attributes are encapsulated in his Sendai Mediatheque for the Northern Japanese city of Sendai, completed in 2001. Containing a series of flexible, evolutionary spaces, the building is essentially a glass cube supported by delicate irregular columns and arches, lending it a characteristic air of fragility.

Ito's conceptual approach has lent itself to a variety of temporary structures and a series of major international exhibitions, but he has also designed some more conventional retail buildings in Tokyo.

As his ideas have slowly become part of the wider architectural landscape, he has finally been commissioned to design major buildings, which are likely to extend his influence further. In 2009, the stunning Main Stadium for the World Games in Kaohsiung in Taiwan created a new morphology for the genre, adopting a snake-like form that opens the arena out to the surrounding area.

Ito's originality, refined use of materials and philosophical experimentation have had an enormous impact on the work of younger architects, especially in Japan. Ito has expressed concern that his influence may have contributed to the establishment of a uniform and vapid kind of minimalism.

Sendai Mediatheque (2001) typifies Ito's transparent and weightless architecture.

Daniel Libeskind

Daniel Libeskind is a high-profile designer of spectacular monumental structures characterised by their fractured appearance. Despite his stature, however, the extreme nature of his architecture has often resulted in controversies, and many of his designs have remained on the drawing board.

Born: 1946, Lodz, Poland
Importance: Leading proponent of Deconstructivist architecture

Born in Poland, Libeskind initially seemed to have a career as a virtuoso accordionist mapped out. His family moved first to Israel, then to New York, where he became a naturalised American citizen and studied architecture.

While well known as an architectural theorist and educator, Libeskind had to wait until his 50s before seeing his first design built. It was, however, a masterpiece. The Jewish Museum in Berlin (completed in 1999) is often described as looking as though it has been hit by a bolt of lightning, which has cracked its solemn, zinc-clad, exterior. The fractured form is highly symbolic, as is the central 'void' around which the museum is built.

Like the 2005 Memorial to the Murdered Jews of Europe in Berlin by compatriot Peter Eisenman, with whom he is often linked, it is architecture that is as much metaphorical as formal. This propensity has led to a string of similar commissions for memorial museums around the world.

Both Libeskind and Eisenman (as well as Gehry) are associated with Deconstructivism, a term that gained currency following an important 1988 exhibition at the Museum of Modern Art New York curated by influential architects Philip Johnson and Mark Wigley. Their description of 'a different sensibility, one in which the dream of pure form has been disturbed' perhaps most closely describes the subsequent work of Libeskind.

These disturbed forms are particularly evident in a remarkable annex to London's Victoria & Albert Museum that Libeskind designed in 2002. It featured dramatic angular shard-like volumes, clad in tile, which seemed to be breaking up. Its extreme appearance polarised opinion between excited adulation and fierce opposition, and the project was abandoned. His slightly more conventional design for Imperial Museum North in Manchester, England, was completed the same year, however.

In 2003, and after a protracted process, Libeskind was selected to master plan the site of the World Trade Center in New York City. His scheme, which he has called the Memory Foundation, is conceived around an ascending circle of skyscrapers. However, he has been increasingly sidelined, and the site's major buildings, including a new transport hub and cultural centre and the main buildings, are to be designed by other leading architects, including David Childs, Norman Foster, Richard Rogers and Frank Gehry.

Libeskind's autobiography, *Break Ground: Adventures in Life and Architecture*, was published in 2004, selling well and being translated into many languages. His legacy will much depend on his ability to develop his style and, more importantly, get his projects through the various planning hurdles required for them to see the light of day.

The fractured form of the Jewish Museum in Berlin (1999) is highly symbolic.

Rem Koolhaas

A dominant figure in the architectural world for the last three decades, Dutchman Rem Koolhaas is as known for his theoretical positions, urban planning concepts, outspoken comments and books as he is for a portfolio of unusual and divergent designs.

Born: 1944, Rotterdam, Netherlands
Importance: Leading theoretical voice in architecture at the start of the 21st century

Koolhaas started out as a writer, producing film scripts and working as a journalist, before studying architecture, which has lent his work its theoretical and polemical nature. After studying in London and Cornell, New York, Koolhaas established his practice OMA, or the Office for Metropolitan Architecture, in Rotterdam in 1975.

He first sprung to fame with his seminal 1978 book, *Delirious New York.* Presented haphazardly as a 'retroactive manifesto' for the city, it outlines an influential vision of New York City as a site of chaos, congestion and irrationality that fundamentally challenged existing urban planning theory. Its massive success was repeated in 1995 with the publication of an enormous tome created together with celebrated graphic designer Bruce Mau. Entitled *S, M, L, XL*, it grouped his various projects by size, accompanied by anything from sketches to seemingly irrelevant little stories.

The success of these books sometimes overshadowed his work as an architect. However, designs such as the Villa D'Ava in Paris (1991), which reinterpreted Le Corbusier's seminal Villa Savoye with a mish-mash of different materials seemingly chaotically thrown together, were major talking points for architects of all persuasions.

Only relatively lately has Koolhaas been asked to design major buildings, such as the Seattle Central Library (2004), with its Deconstructivist spilling glass front, and the eccentrically shaped Casa da Musica concert hall for the city of Porto (2005).

Having both lauded and then later criticised the skyscraper as an architectural and urban form, Koolhaas has, in the 21st century, turned his attentions to designing various important examples. The most significant of these is his design for the headquarters of CCTV, China's state broadcasting company. In the shape of two giant, shiny, leaning towers, connected to form an inverted 'U', it is a deliberate attempt to create an iconic piece of architecture. The subject of local controversy, its completion was delayed by a dramatic fire that was reported around the world, and officially blamed on New Year's fireworks. Koolhaas has suggested that changes in the world economy might make the building, completed in 2009, one of the final moments of an era characterised by 'sensational architectural' statements.

It is difficult to overestimate Koolhaas's influence on contemporary architecture. Many of the most prominent figures have studied with him or worked in his studio, which has acted as a kind of hothouse for young architectural talent. However, his shifting positions and knack for self publicity have also stoked considerable opposition and accusations of fashionable posturing. The extent to which his own name survives in the history books may ironically depend on the building of a single memorable building of the kind his theoretical works have sought to undermine.

The headquarters of CCTV, China's state broadcaster, in Beijing (2009).

Zaha Hadid

One of the most controversial of contemporary architects, Zaha Hadid is known for designing buildings with outlandish sinewy and fluid forms that have pushed accepted notions of architecture to the limit. She is one of the only high-profile women in the world of architecture.

Born: 1950, Bagdad, Iraq
Importance: Highly original architect renowned for creating fluid forms

Iraqi-born Hadid studied mathematics in Beirut before moving on to study architecture in London, working closely with influential architect Rem Koolhaas and becoming a partner in his renowned OMA.

In 1980, she founded her own practice, but while she had a high profile as a teacher in purely architectural circles, her designs were seen as too challenging, usually for technical reasons, and remained on the drawing board. She sprung to prominence in 1994, when her design won the competition to design the Cardiff Bay Opera House. Protracted political wrangling saw the design being shelved, but the attendant media coverage meant that Hadid's name was now on everyone's lips.

Apart from a couple of buildings, including the Vitra Fire Station (1994), Hadid's designs famously went unbuilt until the start of the 21st century, when she was finally able to dispel this reputation as a creator of theoretic

'I started out trying to create buildings that would sparkle like isolated jewels; now I want them to connect, to form a new kind of landscape.'

architecture and major commissions began to flood in. Her studio is now one of the leading global architectural practices, and structures designed by Hadid are being erected around the world. In 2004, she was awarded the Pritzker Prize, the highest honour in architecture.

Hadid's sculptural approach to architecture has tested the limits of current technology, but thanks to exponential increases in the sophistication of architectural and engineering software, many of her ideas became feasible. Her designs often banish straight lines to become instead 'seamless' both in their form and relation to their environment. These are elements evident in her widely admired Bergisel Ski Jump (2002) and also the Nordpark (2007) Cable Railway Buildings, both in Innsbruck, Austria.

Two larger-scale designs that were greeted with widespread critical acclaim are the giant shark-like presence of the Phaeno Science Center in Wolfsburg, Germany (2006), and the Rosenthal Center for Contemporary Art in Cincinnati, Ohio (2003), in which the ground curves upwards to form an 'urban carpet'. Both exemplify an approach that has been termed 'parametricism' by Patrik Schumacher, a longtime collaborator and partner of Hadid.

Hadid has also begun to apply her distinctive formal language to furniture, lighting and even shoes. While her showy designs are starting to be associated with the excesses of the economic bubble of the early 21st century, they remain among the most distinct and original of current architecture. And even though her formidable persona and architecture polarises opinion, every new project emanating from her studio is closely studied by the architectural community and she continues largely to garner the utmost respect from her peers.

The 'seamless' form of the Bergisel Ski Jump, Innsbruck, Austria (2002).

SUSTAINABLE ARCHITECTURE

Sustainable architecture means different things to different people. As important arbiters of the way in which we live, architects have found themselves in the front line, pressed to find new solutions and materials that can respond to the ecological crisis the world is facing.

Many of the materials that had been central to Modernist buildings, such as concrete and asbestos, are now seen are either environmentally unfriendly or hazardous. Likewise, many of the designs are now seen as profligate in their use of energy. As a result, architects have been forced increasingly to take into consideration issues such as energy efficiency, respect for the immediate environment, the use of recycled and/or recyclable materials, and alternative energy sources. Wood, in particular, has made a return as a popular primary building material.

Some green features are more obvious than others, such as green or 'living' roofs, in which the top of the building is covered with turf for superior insulation, its ability to blend with surrounding areas and encourage wildlife. A notable example is the 2008 California Academy of Sciences, in Golden Gate Park, San Francisco, designed by Renzo Piano, which has an undulating verdant roof.

Another prominent trend has been 'reuse', in which architects scavenge and re-purpose discarded materials and

> '*The urgent task is to forge an environmentally responsible modern architecture, to use technology to achieve beneficial ends.*'
>
> Richard Rogers

structures. Groups such as 2012 Architecten in the Netherlands have created modular pods that are constructed out of discarded panels from washing machines, for example. The reuse of shipping containers has created a whole category of 'container architecture'. Important examples include the Freitag store opened in 2006 in Zurich, which creates a mini high-rise store of containers stacked one above another, and the enormous Nomadic Museum (2005), designed by Shigeru Ban, a Japanese architect also known for his integration of paper and cardboard as architectural materials. However, attempts by figures such as American architect Adam Kalkin to redeploy containers and create readymade domestic residences that could be bought off the shelf have been criticised for their expense, and also for providing merely a fashionable gesture rather than a fundamental solution.

While most contemporary sustainable architecture is less extreme, the ecological imperative has spawned a new aesthetic and an attendant industry of consultants and specialist advisers, and this is particularly evident in the case of civic buildings such as schools. Some commentators have argued that sustainability is a matter of building technology and separate from the concerns of architects, but this ignores the fact that the greatest architects of the past – the early Modernists in particular – were able to combine new materials and social changes to create new and innovative structures.

Few architects today would admit publicly to ignoring the issue of sustainability, but they tend to be polarised around one of two approaches. Conventional design processes may be slightly modified to incorporate green elements, while smaller-scale projects adopt a more experimental approach that puts sustainability centre stage. A truly sustainable and viable mainstream approach to design and building has yet to be developed.

Herzog & de Meuron

Swiss duo Jacques Herzog and Pierre de Meuron, are among the most respected contemporary architects, managing to produce works of subtle, inscrutable perfection that impress their peers and yet create iconic statements with popular appeal. They are particularly known for using novel construction techniques and materials.

Born: (Both) 1950, Basel, Switzerland
Importance: Virtuoso architects who employ novel materials to create iconic buildings

Childhood friends, they established the practice of Herzog & de Meuron in their home city of Basel in 1978, producing a series of highly considered buildings characterised by their pared-down forms and distilled perfection, which has led to their work sometimes being described as 'Modernist reductivist'.

Proficiency with materials is another salient feature of their projects – in each, one particular material is exploited to maximum effect. For instance, the de Young Museum in San Francisco (2005) features a mesh-like covering of perforated copper cladding, while the Laban Dance Centre in London (2003) has an exterior of double-skinned polycarbonate (more usually seen on garden sheds or greenhouses), which is subtly lit to create a gentle iridescent effect. On many of their projects, Herzog and de Meuron like to collaborate with outside artists, which contributes to the sculptural quality of their work.

While their work was already widely admired in architectural circles, the design that propelled the duo to popular fame was their conversion of Bankside, a disused Art Deco power station in London, into the new Tate Modern, which opened in 2000.

The Allianz Arena, a football stadium in Munich completed in 2005, was also a triumph. The entire structure was covered in a thin, translucent skin of ethylene tetrafluoroethylene, a special kind of a

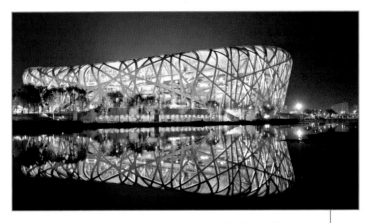

Beijing National Stadium for the 2008 Olympics, dubbed the Bird's Nest.

plastic. This in turn was lit up, its colours dependent on how the stadium was being used and which of the home teams that shared it were playing, creating a spectacular and much photographed effect.

However, their design for the Beijing National Stadium for the 2008 Olympics, designed in conjunction with a large team that included artist Ai Weiwei, managed to be an even greater success. The converse of the Allianz Stadium, it exposes its structure as decoration, leading to its colloquial appellation of the Bird's Nest. Seen and praised by millions around the world, the building has become an icon of the games and of contemporary China.

The practice is the most lauded of contemporary architecture, and its output is closely scrutinised by architectural students. Despite their fame, however, Herzog and de Meuron eschew the celebrity of contemporaneous 'starchitects', instead adopting a stance of haughty aloofness (the practice famously does not even have a website) that has proved equally effective in maintaining a very high profile.

The practice of Herzog & de Meuron is in high demand with clients looking for high-impact statement architecture around the world, and it is currently working on an array of major projects, primarily for cultural institutions, that are likely to cement its reputation for virtuosity yet further.

Index

For main entries see contents page.

For Tom

First published 1983 by Walker Books Ltd
87 Vauxhall Walk, London SE11 5HJ

This edition published 2013

2 4 6 8 10 9 7 5 3 1

This book has been typeset in Veronan light

Printed in China

British Library Cataloguing in Publication Data:
a catalogue record for this book is available from the British Library

ISBN 978-1-4063-4150-8

www.walker.co.uk

Eating Out

Helen Oxenbury

WALKER BOOKS
AND SUBSIDIARIES
LONDON · BOSTON · SYDNEY · AUCKLAND

Mum said, "I'm too tired
to cook."
Dad said, "I'll take you
out for supper."

"I suppose you need a high
chair," the waiter said.
The room was hot and stuffy.

We had to wait ages
for the food.
"Why can't you sit still
like those nice little
children?" Dad said.

"Get back on your chair,"
Mum said. "Here comes
your lovely meal."

"Why didn't you say you wanted to go before the food arrived?" Mum said.

I wasn't very hungry,
so I went under the table.
Someone trod on my foot.

The waiter made
a terrible mess.

"That's that," Dad said.
"Never again," said Mum.
"Anyway, I like eating at
home the best," I said.